THE VOICE OF THE THUNDER

THE VOICE OF THE THUNDER

Laurens van der Post

William Morrow and Company, Inc.
New York

First published in Great Britain by Chatto & Windus in 1993

"The Great Memory" was first published in 1984 under the title "Witness to a Last Will of Man" in *Testament to the Bushmen* by Laurens van der Post and Jane Taylor (Viking).

"The Little Memory" was first published in 1988 under the title "The Great and the Little Memory" in *The Lost World of the Kalahari* by Laurens van der Post, with photographs by David Coulson (Chatto & Windus).

It is the policy of William Morrow and Company, Inc., and its imprints and affiliates, recognizing the importance of preserving what has been written, to print the books we publish on acid-free paper, and we exert our best efforts to that end.

Library of Congress Cataloging-in-Publication Data

Van der Post, Laurens.
    The voice of the thunder / Laurens van der Post.
        p.   cm.
    ISBN 0-688-12951-x
    1. Life.   2. Self (Philosophy)   3. Identity.   4. Van der Post,
Laurens.   I. Title.
BD435.V36   1994
128—dc20
                                                                93-23605
                                                                CIP

Printed in the United States of America

First U.S. Edition

1 2 3 4 5 6 7 8 9 10

To
Maria Magdalena,
my mother

'In that timeless moment there was a flash of the long lightning of Africa and I heard the voice of the thunder that followed and, hard on that, one of those dear Griqua-Hottentot voices, also a fragment of one of the most ancient races of Africa, commanding his fellows to listen, because it was the voice of their God.'

From 'The Other Journey'

Contents

The Other Journey

'Make haste back to the light . . .'
HOMER, *The Odyssey* (Anticleia
to her son, Odysseus, in Hades)

THE PATTERN OF the little memory and the great memory has been with me all my life. In an African sense I have taken it, with what I have written here, perhaps as far as it can be taken. I say 'perhaps' because I am acutely aware of how little I have done, in one way, to record the outer eventfulnesses of my life. These have been many and varied and, I am constantly told, unusual. Friends, publishers and a vast correspondence from readers all over the world have not ceased to ask me for more.

One special, lovable biographer, who among his other books has written the official life of Eugene O'Neill, pressed me so hard to collaborate with him on a biography that our friendship was stressed almost to a breaking point and would have been broken if he had not been a person also of singular understanding and worth. Although I steadfastly declined, and said that I did not have the space of mind or time to collaborate with him, he insisted on proceeding without my help. I told him over and over again I found there was something indecent about recording a person's life before he had lived the full circle of his own ration of time. I emphasized that, as far as there was any objective interest which could be of importance to a larger world and had a special meaning not only for me but for the time in which I lived, I had done all I could do to honour that feeling. Nonetheless, he pursued me from the west coast of America where he lived, and where I thought I had delivered a final and unmistakable 'no' in person, to England and appeared one afternoon without warning at the door of my home in Chelsea.

I was glad to see him in a way, but felt acutely embarrassed and almost angry that I would have to refuse a guest in my house and a friend of long standing the thing he had come to ask me, and a complex of other feelings made normal hospitality seem a poor compensation to offer him.

Yet, despite this final refusal, he went on to see friends of mine in London, to none of whom had I introduced him, travelled to Africa and I do not know where else, returned to his home in California to write the biography, and eventually sent me a copy which I have not read and shall never read.

I do not know if this little happening reflects merit on either of us. I fear it may suggest a certain hardheartedness and lack of feeling on my part, yet I cannot force myself to read the book, because in a sense that would make me what is called in law an accessory after a fact that I had done all I could to prevent. I refer to it here only because it illustrates how wrong I still feel it would be for me to engage in a process of looking back over my shoulder instead of watching my step in the here and now towards what lies unfinished and unlived ahead. The sombre warnings against looking back in all mythologies, from the most primitive stories to the more advanced ones like Lot's wife and Orpheus and Eurydice, never seemed to me fanciful or vain, but warnings which the human spirit and imagination ignored at their peril.

Here I must hasten to add, lest the literal-minded accuse me of flagrant self-contradiction, that there is a vast difference between looking back and remembering. Memory, particularly the memory with which I am concerned, plays an immense, indescribable role in human life, and without it we would have nothing to give life the continuity it needs, and the spirit a container for all that it has experienced of value. It is, in fact, a form of making the past a forever present element of human imagination and being and doing, and is in no sense related to the indulgence of nostalgia and a still unappeased longing to return to things that have vanished forever. It would not be an over-simplification to say that looking back tends to make the present a past, whereas remembering makes what is valid in the past part of the present.

My own predisposition of nature was, I believe, on the whole free in this regard, and made me less interested in the instant sensation values and drama of events than in the 'something else' for which the event was, as it were, a proxy. What became most significant for me was the realization that that 'something' was not of one's own timing but at the disposal of an imponderable which grew of its own accord in one's imagination until in some far-off, unforeseen day it would flower and daze one's senses with its beauty and import and light of meaning, and all that there is of arrogance and presumption in this slanted consciousness of our day would be humbled in a heightened perception of the abuse of its own natural proportions. Or, to use a metaphor which I have orchestrated elsewhere in my writing, the meaning of the event then enters one whole, like the light of those stars to which astronomy so often directs us these days, and amazes our senses centuries of light years after the stars themselves have been born, and on occasion after they themselves have vanished into the outer darkness again.

As a result, the more experienced I became in watching this night sky of my awareness, the more it seemed as if there were a great acausal something intruding between the cause and the effect of events, between two great ends that appear so firmly and blindly shut, linked to the 'becoming'

5

that was the continuity of all creation; and as if, finally, when one moved into what is called the effect, the event was transformed into something more than mere causality could have achieved. From that 'something else' we derived our sense of meaning and direction.

I found myself as a consequence increasingly concerned with the sort of personal astronomy and the quintessence of experience surrounding the sense of meaning held in the trust of what I have called here a little memory, bonded to a greater and indescribable memory before individual time, if not before time itself, and which, known or unknown, seen or unseen, recognized or unrecognized, appeared to be the real plenipotentiary of creation. If this were not so, how could I possibly have been so stirred by the great preliminary of all the stories I ever heard as a child, from the moment my nurse dropped, like a pebble into a very still and clear pond sending ripples outwards and on to all the translucent sensations without shape or name which surrounded one's bed at evening, the phrase 'Once upon a time . . .'

Yes! Oh yes, the feeling was inescapable: 'Once upon a time . . .' one had been somewhere else and been equipped with experience and foreknowledge of what was to come in this awesome dimension and ante-room of space and time one had just entered. As I grew older, proof that I was not alone in this rippling perception came in the testimony of poets, artists and seers, as for instance the Wordsworth who wrote in his ode on immortality:

> Our birth is but a sleep and a forgetting:
> The Soul that rises with us, our life's Star,
> Hath had elsewhere its setting,
> And cometh from afar;

Not in entire forgetfulness,
And not in utter nakedness,
But trailing clouds of glory do we come
From God, who is our home.

Yet even this inspired statement was not without flaw in the context of all that crowded in on me. In particular the line 'Not in entire forgetfulness' seemed almost a shocking understatement for the wordless feelings of a positive remembrance which came over me. It was to prove enough to involve me for the rest of my life in a process of wondering as much about the 'before' and 'after' as the 'now', and more about the unknown spread out like the night sky above one's imprisonment in a cell of the known. I would look at newborn children, for instance, and think not of how young and vulnerable they were, but how old. And from my own experience of living I came to realize that, even if one accomplished the full round of one's allocated span, the best of us would have added little to what life and creation had already invested within us as children.

Paradoxically the adolescent, facing consciously and ill-prepared his own personal birth into life where he would have to assume responsibility for his own nature and be charged henceforth to live it out without deviation and as fully as he could, seemed young and poignantly defenceless, were it not that the remembrances which are automatic in the child insisted on a kind of sleeping partnership with him as he grew older. This kind of sleeping is perhaps what Shakespeare had in mind when, at the end of his own great journey in *The Tempest*, he concluded: 'We are such stuff as dreams are made on, and our little life is rounded with a sleep'. It is also perhaps this sleep to which another great Elizabethan poet and contemporary of Shakespeare, the inspired healer and physician of Norwich, Sir Thomas

Browne, was referring when he declared: 'My body sleeps and my soul awakes'.

This affirmation was of the utmost importance to me, because it caused me to read on and on in that magnificently symphonic essay, *Urn Burial*, which led to discovery of the lines in *Religio Medici*: 'We carry within us the wonders we seek without us: there is all Africa and her prodigies in us.' Thus, from then on, although I did not know it at the time, I was engaged increasingly one way or another in a life that was as much an act of remembrance as of discovery, as much a 'Once upon a time . . .' as it was a 'now', as much and even more than both the 'being' and the 'doing' in the now, obedient to a 'to come' greater than their sum.

And in this regard fate seemed to have singularly blessed me from the moment of birth, surrounding me with living examples of perhaps the oldest forms of human life to which we still have access in the world, and moreover, in the context of that other Africa to which Thomas Browne referred, still charged with the natural wonder and pro-digiousness that the Elizabethan healer found within himself.

I have often thought in this connection of something Jung once told me, and which he subsequently expanded at great length in his writing, that all human beings have a two-million-year-old person within themselves, for I seemed to be accompanied in my most impressionable years by a great variety of neighbours in real life of this ancient of ancients which Jung saw lodged in all life. The consequences were immediate and unending. There was, for instance, the way in which I came to look at birth. I accepted, of course, that birth for everyone born is special, and differs from all other forms of birth. Yet those differences are not competitive, and without fear or favour they remain equal in the order of dignity of creation. This dignity does not preclude that

8

all are different. Here in the preamble of life on earth there is the immutable provision that creation is not a programme in conformity but rather is committed to diversity and to an increase through diversity of new and more and more options and revelations of areas of creation to swell the great flow of becoming to which the stars, the nebulae and the foam and spray of the Milky Way bear witness and quicken the sense of unclaimed realities beyond.

I could not ever therefore ignore the fact that, however inexpressible all this was, the beginning had to have a human face. It was personified in an image of the warmest flesh and blood of a human being, and that human being had a 'Once upon a time . . .' face and a 'Once upon a time . . .' spirit. It was the face of my nurse Klara, to whom I have so often referred in my writing. It was she who was a precious one-some of the last remnants of the first people of Africa, per-haps the oldest form of human life to which we still had access in my day. Had I been born in Australia, perhaps I would have called it by the moving Australian recognition of memory at the beginning, the aborigines' 'dreamtime'. It would be part of the reality which many years later in the Kalahari Desert made a Bushman hunter, when I was ques-tioning him about the stories of their own beginnings, shake his head with passion and say that it was all too difficult to express because 'there is a dream dreaming us'. I obviously must have known my mother's face long before I knew Klara's; yet it was not that of my mother, with whom I had such a long, unique and precious relationship, but Klara's that came first, since my mother's face was more of the 'now' but Klara's of the 'Once upon a time . . .' that was also bonded to a 'Once upon a time . . .' to come.

Pressed recently in the course of a dialogue over many years with a close friend to tell him what final conclusions and feelings I had come to as I approached the end of my life, I found no conclusions that were not as provisional as the others which had preceded them. There were none that could be put into concepts or even the most eloquent of definitions. There were only vast feelings without shape or name, aglow in the rainbow colours, each in its own right, massed after refraction for the great moment of metamorphosis when they could flame into one another and fulfil, out of chaos and old night, that radiance of my first days. With this evocation, even to think of this moment always as a beginning, or a return, seemed to be meaningless. I had always thought of departure and return as the deepest pattern of human life. I had always thought of them in terms of an origin and a destination, and yet in the emotions of this image, which still arises as clear and undimmed as it seemed when it first came into my awareness, beginning and end, origin and destination, had all along been one.

So there it was, irrevocable and unalterable, the deepest pattern in the human spirit was precisely this sort of moon-bonded departure and return that made origin and destination one and is only fulfilled since it no longer excludes what is to come from the heart of the 'now'. T. S. Eliot, in 'Little Gidding', has said it perhaps better than any other poet in his great pledge to life:

> We shall not cease from exploration
> And the end of all our exploring
> Will be to arrive where we started
> And know the place for the first time.

Yet as the echo of this exhortation fades behind us from wall to wall down the Grand Canyon of time, is this really all that there is be said about this pattern? Is this really all that Eliot meant to convey? The echo may well vanish but the question remains: is the spirit, left at this final point of return, not inflicted perhaps with a new unease? Is the moment perhaps not implicit still with a 'something else', another call on the human being, however full of the knowledge gathered in the long years of travel and separation behind it, which cannot be left with the experience as mere knowledge but demands something more?

I have always had a feeling, and now more than ever before, that it is not enough just to know. Somehow, somewhere before the last call for the curtain, before the enlarged recognition of all the knowledge earned in exile and confirmed in reunion not dreamt of at the beginning, something new seems to have crossed the horizon of awareness and inflicted a feeling of a vital 'something missing' on the human scene.

There seemed to be no neat answer or any purely rational way of dealing with this kind of wondering. There was only the ancient and proven way of returning to the symbols and images which rise of their own accord in the imagination, and flower and bear fruit in the myths and legends and stories that have accompanied us from the moment of our separation from that which created us, on and up to this desperate and confused moment where we stand today.

So I found myself at this point over and over again returning to Homer's *Odyssey*, and in particular to the reunion at Ithaca when Odysseus and Penelope make themselves known to each other at last, when departure and return, destination and origin, have most clearly become one, and the moon of the masculine and feminine in life is full again and overflowing. There, I was shocked into remembering, the story is not ended; the journey is not over. What could possibly be the 'more' that life is asking of this flesh and blood? They had both lived and endured all that fate had inflicted upon them, without diminishing the meaning and significance of their spirit, and so wholly

11

qualified themselves for the readiness of Eliot's recognition of the places of departure in the human pilgrimage as if for the first time. If they were not ready for ceasing from exploration, what then?

I could only look again at the moment in that strange visit to Hades which Odysseus had been compelled to make and thus to break away from his main reach for home. It is a point where, however much without size or substance, Odysseus's life and the journey ahead must be repositioned, so that the greatest story, in which the story of himself and Penelope is included, can be brought to its proper end. The blind seer Teiresias sets out the course that he is to follow, plain as an Admiralty chart. He described in detail Odysseus's journey to come, and all that has to be done before he can rejoin Penelope and bring law and order back to the disintegrating Ithaca. It is all there in awesome and dramatic detail, but this 'end beyond the end' may strike the imagination of Homer's listeners as still too remote and indefinite to be of immediate consequence. It may appear that after leaving Hades Odysseus sails on to the most exciting and dangerous part of his journey, because more than ever he is now alone. All his ships have been shattered and wrecked by storms, almost all caused by his sins against the gods and their laws of proportion. Odysseus's fate has never been more properly and heavily unloaded onto himself and his own indomitable spirit and behaviour, and what with the drama of this and the other great eventfulnesses which preceded this sombre meeting in Hades, Teiresias's prophecy fades in the recesses of the reader's memory, but it is never lost. It is lodged deep in the mind of Odysseus, not inert but like lava of a volcano asleep. In the moment when he and Penelope have made themselves known to each other, and accepted what they have always been to each other since the beginning, the memory erupts and Odysseus is compelled to tell her at once about the prophecy of this other journey.

But before he completes the account it is almost as if he is appalled by what he is doing, that he appears to have come home only to tell Penelope that he has got to go away again. Perhaps aware how unfeeling and insensitive all this must seem, he interrupts himself and says that the detail can be left until later. Penelope refuses to accept that, and insists that he should finish the tale. Both these things are told in simple sentences without any rhetoric or licence, and their very simplicity and starkness make them all the more impressive, because nothing reveals more clearly how deep is the need for the truth, and how nothing now but the truth can be food for two such spirits purified in the fire of their purgatorial years of suffering and separation.

And so, for an instant, one is compelled to contrast what is happening with something that took place long before the union we are now witnessing, something inconceivable before the descent into Hades, the extreme layer of the collective unconscious of man as a modern interpretation would have it, the dimension where all life's greatest energies are stored and where, quite apart from making a dutiful return to the spirits of the ancestors, Odysseus turns to his mother, the abiding image of the element in the human spirit which bears and brings forth and never fails life's need of recreation. This is the way of last and first resort, and if it does not succeed, nothing else will restore in him the will and direction to get home again. So much has gone wrong before. There is still so much in front to go wrong, and the odds against his survival appear as insurmountable as ever.

All this comes at one as a fleeting sense of the apparent enormity of what Odysseus is doing to Penelope. One almost turns against this man who has suffered so much, because of this ostensible brutal insensitivity. How could he – one is tempted to join in the process of censure which Odysseus himself had to overcome – come home to say, without preamble or apology to his woman, who has suffered as much in her own lonely way as he in his, that he has just come home to go away again? The temptation vanishes almost as soon as it comes, and with it all traces of censure.

They vanish because what all the imagery and myth and legends and most inspired visions of life have taught us is that the height to which the spirit can rise is matched only by the depth to which it has descended into the darkness within itself. Though the longing in the listener and hearer for some euphemism of all this imagery of return could not be greater or more compelling, and the Siren voices within the human heart still suggest that by now men must have learnt how to improve upon the truth, the symbol and images do not yield or fail. The temptation is, for those who listen truly, just another example of the rationalism and intellectualism of our time, wherein reasons for supporting a subversive underground evasion of the truth are among the most inventive, plausible and tempting to which the spirit of the day is inclined. Deep in life there is a code of grace that truth cannot do without; there are moments when compassion calls for a certain diplomacy of truth before the whole can be exposed, naked and unashamed. But this is not such a moment. This truth, this kind of right of the truth, which this man and woman have earned on the long journey and separation behind them, has no need of any graces, has no need for being slowly unfolded and retarded for some sentimental moment for its delivery. It is a truth which is inseparable from its illumination, and it would be as vain to try to separate thunder and lightning, because in it life has been made immediate. It is an immediacy in which nothing false can enter, and in its coming there in Ithaca the only words that can serve it strike as pure as lightning and as a direct descendant of 'the word that was in the beginning', as clear and commanding as thunder.

It has to be so because this is the point of no return, the only position feasible if the pattern of creation is to be truly fulfilled. Up to now, all the separation and suffering that had been imposed on Odysseus and Penelope had, as it were, been shown in terms of outer eventfulnesses and circumstances and their duty to communion and neighbouring of humanity and perceptions of their future. All they had to endure was part of them which belonged to the common lot of a man and woman of a specific moment of that time, and which had to be undertaken with untried and partial selves not yet knowing in full what they were doing. But here, before the curtain on the last act is lifted, one knows that, whatever is to come, they are to be pledged with all and more of themselves. The moment is here, to put it in the language of contemporary philosophy, the moment when what has been unconsciously lived is made conscious, when the collective is about to be made specific, the universal become individual and re-neighboured, and flesh and blood enabled to rise in dignity and commitment to the highest estate of life, and discover the emancipation and the freedom which are only to be found when with all their heart and mind they embrace and surrender themselves with love to the will of creation.

This then is the significance and testimony of the new and final urgency of those long years of suffering and separation. Their account is about to be rendered, a great debt to life discharged, and the book closed. So, despite the turmoil and battles that await Odysseus only a few unforgiving hours away, however plausible the voices may have been in him to postpone the rest of the account of his meeting in Hades, he accepts that he has to tell Penelope he has another journey to make. So, brief and stark, he tells her what Teiresias has told him, and she without a moment's hesitation accepts that what has been decreed by the gods must be fulfilled, and that no doubt the gods who decreed it will take care of them, as they have taken care of them up to now.

It is, for me, one of the most moving moments in *The Odyssey*. Like the descent into Hades and the meeting with Nausicaa, the image of his own feminine soul in its purest, unblurred and most evocative form, here, with the truth in himself in command, it is as if the feminine which was so implicit and pure in Nausicaa faces him in Penelope in its mature form, as if she had just stepped from her flame on the mountain of the purgatory which those twenty-one years behind her must now appear to have been. Indeed, as one listens again to this great song, reverberating with undiminished power over those long millennia, one walks with Homer on this immense search for wholeness and meaning.

And if one still has any inclination to think of this as exaggerated, one has just to imagine what would have happened if Odysseus had withheld this element of his return from the woman Penelope had become, and waited for some ostensibly more appropriate moment, possibly weeks after his return, to tell her. A new golden thread would have snapped and been withdrawn from the pattern which Penelope had woven into that loom of fate which was her only sure defence against the falseness and the counterfeit of the world.

And there is proof positive too in the way the day itself comes to an end. The long, level light of evening glides over the rim of the world, and the world itself seems to fall away from them. The bustle, and even the sound of footfall, vanishes as the special story of Odysseus and Penelope, in their two separate and distinct selves, fulfils itself in a union that is so much greater than the sum of their individual parts could ever have been without the separation and the suffering of the spent years behind them. All has been done and well done between them, and they have been made as ready as human beings can ever be ready for what is over all and beyond.

Now Homer, the blind poet and singer of the song, who is eyeless in life, Teiresias-like, to see more clearly within, as always when intensity of meaning is at its greatest, soars to render himself at his simplest, and completes this provisional final phase, this intermediate end, with the unadorned words: 'The women have been sent away to rest. It is dark and the great house is silent, and those two could enjoy at last the blessing of their love.'

One can imagine what modern writers would have made of such a reunion, and the horror of the realistic parade of detail. But, like the truth which Homer himself never seeks to improve upon, this is the Euclidian point of their story where there can be no substance or magnitude of words but position only for the deed that is sheer poetry within itself. It is a moment comparable to that when Shakespeare realizes that his descent with Hamlet on one of the greatest journeys into the antarctic winter of the unconscious can go no further, and that the prince who suffered so much in the cause of human awareness has earned his rest also in the mind of his creator, and that there is no more to be said than a 'Goodnight, sweet prince.'

So this prince and princess, after their good goodnight, arise refreshed and ready for the battle which has to be fought to make Ithaca itself and whole again, and free Odysseus finally from his duties to the world as king and man, for the final initiation and eucharist of his own and Penelope's greater selves. There is time just between the account of the awakening and the battle in the great hall to remember how it all began, with a dream sent from Olympus into the head of Agamemnon sleeping by his black ship on the beachhead of Troy; to recall the great numbers of kings and princes and heroes and their women who have suffered and died on the great plain of Ilium; and to reflect that the real glory of it all was not on the battle fields, the seas in which they had perished or the vile intrigues and feuds that laid them low, like Agamemnon himself, when they had more than earned their return. Rather, the real purpose all along had been to earn their discharge from collective unreality and to achieve a more meaningful union of man and woman through their differentiation which is beyond even the battle about to come. For the only victory in this epic of searching and suffering is in the making of man and woman as totally themselves and also totally one, with this oneness itself committed to joining creation on the greatest journey of all towards an awareness which has not yet been achieved on earth. This is the moment of the real triumph of God and man, and of the greater over the lesser meaning. Odysseus and Penelope walk into battle with a light upon them that had not been seen before on the desperate Homeric scene, leading one of the greatest mythological cavalcades ever dreamt of in the story of life on earth with a step that will resound forever in the heart and mind of man.

The battle itself then is fought with an intensity which threatens to revive the spirit of killing with which Odysseus had sailed from Troy and which had nearly undone his voyage home before it had properly started, with that senseless raid and plunder of an innocent island on his way. Indeed it is so great that Pallas Athena, the most differentiated of all the goddesses on Olympus, is in danger herself of being overcome. In extravert terms it is as exciting a phase as any in *The Iliad*, all the more so because the people most involved have become intimates in the house of the readers' and listeners' imagination after the twenty-one years of their lives on which Homer had reported with such inspiration. Even the great cloud-gatherer, Zeus, becomes so alarmed by the ferocity of the battle and the way it threatens to spread that he intervenes and brings the fighting to an end with the greatest of his thunder and lightning, so immediate and together that Homer describes them as 'a blazing thunderbolt'. Only through this divine intervention are the spent years redeemed and all that the spirit of Odysseus has gained is there to serve the renewal of life in Ithaca and its consolidation before he is ready for the journey foretold by Teiresias.

The collective imperviousness in the spirit of European man, which still makes him ignore the fact, let alone the meaning, of the other journey that has now to come, is all the more stubborn because of the climate of the time in which we live and its failure to recognize how quintessentially *The Odyssey* is a religious story. Europe has made a terrible kind of spiritual totalitarianism out of Christianity. It has regarded all other gods and forms of religion as lesser breeds without the laws and commandments of the one and only God it professes to worship. The word 'pagan' for the vast religious dimension of other cultures and peoples may, at its best, be allowed to rise to a certain instinctive form of nobility but is normally denied the dignity of being anything except superstitious and falsely religious.

Yet no people in history were more religious in their own awareness of that ultimate dimension than the Greeks. Wherever they went they were accompanied by their gods. Their gods walked the streets of Athens and Corinth. They kept company with the meanest of citizens and the loneliest of shepherds. They were in the woods, the rivers, on the mountains and even among the stars, and travelled to far-fabled and enchanted countries as divine pioneers of the great urge to explore the world within the world without which was so fundamental a characteristic of the Greek spirit. There was not an area of life not peopled for the Greeks by gods. So in this coming of peace to Ithaca, as in the past wherever Odysseus had been and had suffered, the gods were present. Called or not called, they were always there. So it is not surprising, as it is most fitting, that the old end and the new beginning in Ithaca is decided religiously by the greatest god of all with his thunder and lightning.

It is at this point of divine intervention that my own pattern seems in some sort related in its lesser way to the overall Odyssean pattern which I believe is, known or unknown, in the unconscious of every human being. The proof of it for me is that this larger pattern has always held my attention, and the older I have grown the nearer it seems to bring me to my own point of departure from the condition which Wordsworth called 'forgetfulness' and the 'sleep' of the child, into the world of the here and now and linked not only to the antique face and the feminine with which I began but also to another sunset moment with Klara when I was first aware of the long lightning of Africa striking, and the thunder spoke deep and long and the sky and earth around my bed on the stoep trembled. In the silence of a rising storm, overawed by the power and majesty of the sound, I heard a Hottentot voice calling on his god, Heitse-Eibib, that god which he would see coming back bleeding in the red of dawn after the battle for light against dark in the night, and whose gentler voice he heard by day as it stirred the acacia leaves and rustled the long camelthorn beans overhead and travelled on to move through the grass at dewfall in the evening with a swish as of silk. 'Heitse, brothers!' the voice called out to his fellow Griquas, the last clan of his kind in the land. 'Heitse! Listen! The Old Master speaks!'

And this indeed was all really that I could tell the friend with whom I had the dialogue about feelings of conclusion in the Eliot sense, not in words so much as in the natural imagery of the occasion which was so clearly a coming home to the beginning and the seeing of it with such increased clarity and intensity as to make first last and last first. Not only did it seem to me to explain that, in one way or another, my life had been a process of listening of that kind, but it was only now, towards the end of the pattern, that the full symbolic meaning of these greatest of natural phenomena seemed revealed to me. Lightning was the awareness imperative, the summons of creation to all life – and above all human beings – to renew and increase themselves and their awareness. It was the awareness which could not be denied because it was the object of the ultimate longing of all creation. The older I became, the more the intimation grew that the deepest longing in the universe of the unconscious, in fact the greatest of all the urges in the collective unconscious, was this strange, irresistible longing to become more conscious: that, and not the unconscious, was the real life-giving mystery. Consciousness, as we know it, is said to be comparatively new, and that, we are told, is why it is, in a sense, frail and vulnerable, however great its appearances of power over matter. But I never found this theory convincing, no matter how much authority it derived from backing by great scientists and psychologists. Of course one had no idea where creation began; but I had a deep, strange feeling, which gave me hope and direction in my own life, that at a moment in time when creation

21

too was only that which as yet has no size and magnitude but only position, this position was a longing and a pledge of all there was of energy and striving and courage and indeed love at the beginning, the child of the raging wind that was Eros, to make that which was unconscious conscious, and that for life on earth this longing, this undismayable imperative announced itself, whenever a new stage in awareness was called for, in the natural symbolism of lightning and its inseparable twin, the word that was thunder.

Thunder was the 'word in the beginning' and the sign that the sentence so begun had to be written out, and lived until the end, if end there was in more than the arbitrary limits imposed on it by human senses, although I do not think that I would have understood it now even a fraction as well if it had not been for Klara's 'Once upon a time . . .' face and being with which it was associated. She too was most obsessed with thunder and lightning and influenced me to be likewise. It made no difference that the timing of this first recollection of thunder came to me later than my awareness of the feminine face, because the meaning with which the realization was concerned is outside time and place. All that increases our consciousness of meaning shares always the same moment in the chronology of meaning whenever it occurs. It was another sign that I had already moved from the 'sleep' and 'forgetting' with which Wordsworth blazed the trail of his own poetic utterance. It was a proof of reality, therefore, that just as there was an interval between the reunion at Ithaca and the beginning of the last battle and its end in thunder and lightning, there was an interval, bridged only by meaning, between my own feelings of conclusion and rediscovery of the voice of 'the word at the beginning'. All that was surprising to me was that I had had to travel so far in years from my first experience of the eventful symbols to what seemed a total apprehension of their meaning, given my own living experience of the vital role that lightning and thunder had played in our lives in the interior of Africa, year after year demonstrating their meaning in action all around us.

There were, for instance, those years marked with long periods of lack of rain and occasions when these were so protracted that they came near to bringing life as we knew it to an end. I could remember the fear and the unbearable anguish which the drought of 1911 – when I was barely four years old – brought not only to the earth but into my own being. This drought was clearly not just part of the external world, hurting the land, killing sheep and cattle and the toughest of wild animals, and turning the veld into a Dead Sea of scorched land, but it was in my own blood and scorched spirit, and made me feel that I would die of a thirst beyond thirst myself, if the rain did not soon come.

When I heard the distant sound of the first thunder from below the horizon and saw it announce its presence in long sweeps of lightning through the dark, the inrush of hope and sense of promise brought back into a hopeless moment of life was almost unbearable and could have been overwhelming were they not immediately balanced by a fear that the clouds might vanish again as they had often done, and the rain still not come. By this time our sheep and cattle were so weak that they could no longer walk and move from the places where they lay, the sheep with muffled, moaning little bleats breaking from them from time to time, adding a bleak sound to a bleak scene. We had to take their ration of water and food to them, each and every one – a task which went on from dawn to dusk through those burning fiery days. Happily the rains did come just in time and the battle of the earth deep down for survival,

23

like the battle for the renewal of Ithaca, ended with thunder and lightning.

And that, even in a normal season, was how the rain would come, first the lightning, then the thunder and the word calling for the redeeming rain to come, and then the miracle of the rain itself in action, almost like a long lost lover come back taking the Penelope land again in his arms. And the response of the earth in the flowers and grasses and increase of life was immediate, and one's spirit could sing and dance again.

But the first of the thunder and lightning was always high, wild, savage and frightening. Every year people in our part of the land were killed by lightning. Yet long before I learnt at school that lightning was electricity, and all else physics had to say about it, I caught the symbolic 'other' from Klara, for whom it was a pure phenomenon of the spirit. While the women of our community on their different farms would fold up the silver and metal in the house in sheets and blankets in the belief that otherwise they would attract the lightning, hanging towels over all the mirrors and drawing the curtains in their haste, Klara would sit with me on our great verandah and make me look at the lightning because she said that every human being had the same light as the lightning in his eye, and the fiercer the lightning outside, the brighter the light with which the eyes must look directly, steadily and without swerving, back at the lightning. She believed that if the light in one's own eyes did not respond and flare all the brighter because of the example of the lightning, there was a form of lightning that would go black and invisible, and that that form of lightning was the lightning that killed.

This was for me one of the earliest and most convincing illustrations of how symbolic the Bushman spirit was, how rich in the primordial wisdom stored up in that two-million-

24

year-old being of which Jung spoke to me later, describing
it as 'a living treasure of all the experience and knowledge
gained since the beginning of time', and warning that if one
lost touch with this innermost source and its symbols, life,
rootless and adrift on the tides of fate, would fail and die.
Fairly early in my life, thinking of the Bushman symbolism
as I had done from the beginning, I thought of the lightning
and the light in the Bushman eye staring back at the lightning as images of consciousness and awareness, and I ended
up where I still stand today by thinking of lightning as the
call to the battle for increase of awareness which is the
imperative in creation. So that the appearance of Zeus with
his thunder and lightning in Ithaca was for me the proclamation of a great new imperative in the spirit of Odyssean
man, and the thunder kin of the 'word at the beginning'
that was already with Teiresias in Hades. And I could not,
I believe, ever have developed the sense of the unfailing
continuity of life that I still seem to possess, in spite of the
fragmentation that wars and erosions of natural symbolism
in the imagination of modern man have inflicted on it, not
only undamaged but reinforced.

This then was the pattern between my own sense of end
and beginning, a beginning which shines for me now even
brighter and with more meaning in the imagination than it
did in that 'Once upon a time . . .' moment in the interior
of Africa. This threesome was continuous and constant: the
face, the vision of the antique feminine of the 'Once upon
a time . . .' already lit with the light of a 'Once upon a
time . . .' to come; the lightning, ambassador for the awareness imperative which transcends the total awareness of
man and woman united, an awareness of creation itself
which breaks through the inhibitions and limitations of
mere human imagination when it has exhausted itself and
threatens to stand still and retrogress; and the thunder,

direct descendant of the word that was in the beginning, conveying the new redeeming and renewing word to the spirit which seemed to have run dry and lost its meaning and direction because it had not followed the commandment of the first people to see and to listen and accordingly to hear and remember and follow thereafter. How great, therefore, this failure and how deep and obstinate the causes in a rootlessness of the Western spirit, through its break with Jung's 'two-million-year-old person' in itself, is painfully obvious in the fact that for so many years the world of scholars and lovers of the Homeric epic have, for all their love, ignored the Teiresian aspect of *The Odyssey*.

This, of course, is the apex and summit of the universal failure which expresses itself so commonly, and in a way so obviously, to anyone open to the symbols and natural images which seek to inform us of the deeper and as yet undiscovered meaning of life and knowledge of ourselves. A glaring example is the growing distance between the word, the everyday word, and the image which once gave birth to the word; between the memory and the loss of remembrance which is so bleak and stark a feature of the consciousness of modern man. This is not a mere subjective observation of a sort of final round-up of nearly a century of living, but something that a vast number of people are already remarking on. There has never been so much talk, indeed, as there is today about the loss of history and the growing indifference to such awareness of history as there is left. It is almost as if the world is no longer interested in its 'before and after', only in what is of the instant, what is of the day, regardless of its history, its yesterday and tomorrow.

It is, moreover, an amnesia not only of this sort of 'Once upon a time . . .' history of life that has been my special concern in following the pattern of the little and the great memories as I do in the pages that follow, but of the traditional history of mankind everywhere, despite the fact that this sort of history is to human societies what memory is to the individual, and a fundamental element in awareness from which the ordered continuation of the life of man on earth depends. There is, in fact, in the collective dimensions of our time, such a vast loss of memory, and confusion in what little memory is left, that increasingly our societies are as stricken as human beings confined in dreadful isolation in specialist homes, because conscious contact between them and the life of their time has broken down. The psychologist-in-depth in his consulting room, confronted with this phenomenon of memory thus contracted, speaks with alarm of 'dissociation of consciousness', senile dementia, Alzheimer's disease, and gives it other frightening pathological labels, unaware that the society and spiritual structure of life he serves is inflicted with contractions of awareness to an even more alarming degree than the patient with whom he is concerned, and whose plight could easily have been rendered more intractable because of the increase in collective unawareness which surrounds him. Of course the mind too, like all things physical, grows old, but this does not cause the kind of loss of memory with which this pattern is concerned. This growing-old of the mind may appear to be a loss of memory, but if closely and naturally followed and observed it is a creative shedding of all that has become irrelevant in the past, and a vital change of priorities in the memory.

Leaving apart the extent to which great histories at their best are due for a profound reappraisal, the vital process of the feeling of continuation in the spirit of man between his 'now' and his 'Once upon a time . . .' which it served, to however fallible an extent, has almost gone, for our history is not only a record of dynasties and civilizations, of

27

kings and queens, presidents and commissars, and dramatic outer eventfulness. In its deepest level it is also a rollcall of the spirit which, when all recorded memory fails, is linked to the legendary story of man; and when the legendary fails, it is linked to the mythological, where the mythological at last is confronted, where the imagination of man can go no further and, at its best, the great unknown presents itself with a certain kind of transparency in the darkness of unknowing all around us, whence the first intimations of the 'Once upon a time . . .' memory appear and the sense of birth, rebirth and creation marshal the energies at the disposal of the great pattern of departure and return for launching the human being, properly equipped, into his 'now'.

For all the natural doubt that surrounds one in this age, I could not write this with conviction were it not for what, although I cannot define it verbally, illustrates itself with this image of listening to the thunder, watching the lightning, and remembering the face and 'Once upon a time . . .' being which went with the face at my own beginning. I did not do so consciously. I neither understood nor fully realized – and those responsible for my upbringing understood and realized even less – why my life was not lived with a given plan. The pattern came from somewhere else that was not in the mind of any given human example or conventions of people and their societies. Yet it was there, to use another image, like an invisible hand on a tiller, holding an apparently unmanned craft steadily before the wind.

From time to time there were strange intrusions that I could not explain or in any degree evaluate and yet, like the listening to the thunder, played their part in the overall direction. For instance, there was a cloudless morning, with the blue of the day stretched without intimation of cloud

28

or mist from horizon to horizon, when I was walking on the far side of the river at home with my gun in my hand and my dog beside me, listening to the call of some wild fowl deeper in the brush. There could have been no scene more frank and honest and innocent to welcome a boy of seven to an adventure of his own. And then suddenly, in less than a second, it was shattered.

There was an enormous flash of lightning, a phenomenon constantly and proverbially referred to as the ultimate image of the unexpected – a bolt from the blue. I do not know to this day whether there was thunder. I do not think so, because I only remember that my dog yelped and we both turned about and ran as fast as we could, home for shelter in the dark of the house battened down against a sweltering summer's day. It was beyond any explanation, so much so that I never mentioned it to others until recently. But somewhere inside myself I realized with a great sense of fear that it was a sign of great import, perhaps a sign of my own private and personal portion of the awareness imperative of creation. I could orchestrate this now, with hindsight, but I leave it at that, and just add that it lived on and influenced the whole climate of my imagination, in the company of other great revelations about meanings gathered from poets and prophets and men of inspiration. For instance, there was a day when I came across Lear's utterance to Cordelia:

> And take upon's the mystery of things,
> As if we were God's spies

and the question instantly arose, was this perhaps the sign that I too was being marked out to be such a spy? The bolt from the blue was with me again when I heard my grandfather's last reading from his family Bible, the great

State Bible as it was called in my country. He read from the Old Testament the account of Samuel, when he was a mere apprentice in the Temple, hearing in the night a voice calling 'Samuel! Samuel!' The moment I heard it, it struck me with immense awe, as something that I would always remember. Yet the real impact came only that night when I was in the dark, sleeping outside as I mostly did, and looking at the Milky Way with a clear vision both of Orion and the great black hole which we called the entrance to hell, and very clearly I heard a voice as from somewhere far beyond calling 'Samuel! Samuel!' And it was as if the whole of the star-filled night were a temple, and I a Samuel who should respond with an immediate: 'Here am I!' To this day I have only to think of it, let alone write it down, and the original emotion is there, laced with feelings of guilt that I have not responded fully yet.

There were many other and subtler illustrations of how the enrichment of one's imagination came not only from the rational faculties in oneself but from profound non-rational sources, from somewhere else, from behind and through this transparency on the frontier of one's aware-ness, like a kind of radar always keeping one's feelings of origin and destination in a direction that made them one, so that when there came this moment of an apparent absolute return where one ceases from exploration, something else, something other presents itself. A score or more years ago, after its first intimation, I called it 'Odysseus's other jour-ney', but now I know I must call it 'Odysseus's real journey', to which all the travel and traffic of *Iliad* and *Odyssey* and even *Aeneid*, all re-focussed in Odysseus's own pilgrimage before his return to Ithaca, had merely been essential tribu-taries.

Why, one might ask, if this were the real journey did Homer leave it as a prophecy? Why did he not describe it in detail as only he could have told it? Could not his force of imagination and power of song and depth of inspiration have moved the minds of men more than this factual prophecy of Teiresias? And just as he himself was reported to have nodded, could not Teiresias too have nodded and the journey not have taken place? Or was it all just due to the banal fact that Homer might have died before he could do more to the Odyssean theme? This last consideration is instantly dispelled for me because the internal evidence suggests that, whatever happened, Homer would not have done more. He himself, I believe, provides the answer in the emphasis which he puts as nowhere else in the vastness of detailed reporting in *The Iliad* and *The Odyssey*, on Teiresias's prophecy, repeating it twice, and elevating it to an importance and urgency which even the reunion with Penelope and the imminence of the battle to come cannot push into the background.

So it is almost as if Homer's silence is evidence of his profound intuitive respect for what is truly individual in man, and the imagination of everyone who has heard his great song up to this point should now, with little memory and great memory joined, follow and interpret Odysseus's journey unaided for himself. With some such acceptance of the meaning of the ending of *The Odyssey*, one realizes for the first time the significance of why all through the prelude to *The Iliad, The Iliad* itself, and then the journey back to Ithaca, this epic of individuation and search for wholeness in individual man could only have had as its subject, object and instrument an island prince like Odysseus, no other image than a man who personified the highest of 'island values'.

Donne, among the many unforgettable perceptions that go through the imagination like falling stars in the night, said: 'No man unto himself is an island. We are all part of

31

the main.' It is true and it is not true. Every man, in so far as he is part of humanity, is part of the main, provided that main is seen as the sea. The sea is the greatest image accessible to us of the collective unconscious which all men share, and the island as 'a piece of land surrounded by water', as the schoolboy definition puts it so perfectly, is an image of how in this sea there is this stubborn grit of man, conscious of a unique self, a self-contained element which cannot be dissolved, whose task it is, no matter what the storms unleashed against it, to preserve its island earth and stand fast within it for the rest of its time. We are all born with an island heart, however much we are joined to the main unconsciously in the beginning, but with this consciousness, for which the unconscious longs so profoundly, and is contracted to live out by nature, so that at the end of our turn on earth we are joined to the main also consciously. So, being consciously part of the main, it is inevitable and right that the battle for the greater self should begin with a battle and the search for a valid collective self, and when that is attained, as it was symbolically, for example, with the fall of Troy and the restoration of the feminine to its lawful masculine in Menelaus, King of Sparta, it is as if the unconscious realizes the limitations of a mere collective awareness, with its provisional and approximate nature, and demands that it should be made more precise as well as widen its range through the enlargement of the awareness of the individual, which is its one and only frontier in this, the full enterprise of all creation.

So in *The Iliad* the first stage is presented in all the imagery of war, the second stage inevitably in the imagery of the Odyssean journey to Ithaca, to the island which stands fast within its own shape and reality in the vast sea of becoming around it. For the moment it had lost its king, its higher self, because of his absence on duty to the great collective of mankind, and had come near to the point of disintegration when Odysseus, with the unyielding logic which the patterns of the unconscious alone possess, is compelled to start his journey home, to the conclusion we all know. And yet where that conclusion is not enough – what then? Successful as Odysseus and Penelope have been in fulfilling the call for their island wholeness, the island and all the scattered and fragmented world of the great confederation of princes and kings and heroes that have fought the first great battles on the plain of Troy will yet perish if all this is not dedicated to something more than the highest achievement realized in Ithaca after the battle. This is the moment of realization that indeed all would be lost which was so dearly and tragically gained if the individual island selves and fragments of consciousness are not rejoined consciously and at one as part of Donne's main. This is the charge laid upon Odysseus by the gods. This is the logical progression after the return to his full island self, for which life has prepared and designated him.

And for all Homer's silence on the matter, and the failure of some three thousand years to recognize its inevitability, we must accept that Odysseus faithfully performed the Teiresian journey. This other journey that faced Odysseus is part of the inescapable pattern of the human spirit set on the path of individuation and the realization of a self in which the 'I' and the 'thou' in man meet. It is part of Homer's greatness that he leaves us in advance with his record of the journey which Odysseus performed in symbols and imagery. However great and inspired his own detailed version of the journey to come would have been, it would have always been singularly his, particularly after the preconditioning imposed upon those who had listened and heard his song for so long. It is as if in this profound intuitive perception of man's contract with life he knows that he had come to a point where the individual must not be led by others; men have had enough of leaders and should be mature now, ready as they will ever be to make their reckoning with life, each on his own. The poet has done all that he can do for others, giving them human examples that so far have not failed themselves and their quest. He has given them the directions of as infallible an element as possible of what is truly prophetic in the human soul, and a legacy of the little and the great memories fulfilled. It seems to me there is something most moving in the thought that this great imagination, which stands out like a K2 of the Himalayas in the dawn of the Western spirit behind us, could have withdrawn with an implication of delicacy and modesty so effortless as to seem to fall from him like the petal of a rose which has bloomed in full.

Among the few examples I know of imaginations that have felt compelled to take on the Odyssean journey after Ithaca, there is only one that has kept company with Homer and found the real meaning of *The Odyssey* in the imagery of the Teiresian journey. The others seem to me to fail what Homer tried to evoke in human imagination and spirit with that other journey. Even Dante, whom I have loved and read repeatedly since I was a boy, got it wrong, although he got it wrong with merit and dignity and had ample excuse in that he only knew the Roman, that is the extended Trojan, version of *The Odyssey*. He had no Greek, and in so far as he read the story of Odysseus it was the Latin accounts of Ulysses. Even as a child, when I knew far less even than the little I know today, I was horrified that Dante had confined his Ulysses in Hell. The only redeeming feature was that he was confined to Hell with a certain dignity and pagan nobility, and was there not because he denied the final sense of the journey on within himself, but because he set about it in the wrong way.

The one person I know who pursues the journey faithfully is Helen Luke, the author of what I think is the best book on Dante, *Dark Wood to White Rose*, who has done so much for interpreting the myths and legends of Greece in a contemporary way. In a book of essays called *Old Age*, she completes the Teiresian journey truly, rendering it like a contemporary Penelope, weaving its pattern in a home-spun way on a loom designed to keep the false and counterfeit at bay until Odysseus comes home to the ultimate meaning of his story. There may well be others who have done something likewise. I am not a scholar and cannot tell for certain. But thanks to her I had company at last in the way the journey had been fulfilled in my own imagination and felt at last that I had some evidence to support objectively what I had for so long carried as a lone but cherished experience of my own.

I accept therefore that, some time after Zeus's thunder and lightning and the restoration of peace in Ithaca, there comes a moment when Odysseus realizes he can no longer postpone the Teiresian part of his journey. In the Helen Luke version he is depicted as having become unusually preoccupied and somewhat moody, and Penelope increasingly concerned about him. This, of course, is not in the prophecy but it seems to me more than probable because from the moment of his return and the completion of their reunion in Ithaca one no longer encounters Odysseus and Penelope as separate individuals but rather an Odysseus plus a transcended Penelope, and a Penelope with a transcended Odysseus. For after this reunion and this journey in search of the feminine within the masculine which has been Odysseus's unique charge, and makes his story perhaps the greatest story ever told in this regard, man and woman are no longer a twosome, however closely joined, confronting their destiny on earth, but a foursome of the one in the other plus the other in the one. It foretells, of course, a tremendous revolution in the spirit of the human race and a profound evolutionary trend which has not yet come to its climax but is breaking into the consciousness of the twentieth century with increased power and frequency. It means that the new relationship implied between men and women has become infinitely more complex and profound, and so of far greater potential for creation in the future. So it is not surprising that when, in the Helen Luke version, Odysseus is overcome at last by the feeling that he can no longer delay the journey foretold in Hades, there is a surge of joy which passes mere desire in both of them as Odysseus tells her that he is setting forth on the Teiresian quest without further delay.

From here, provided one abandons the dimensions of the literal and the arid, rational ideologies of our time and confines oneself to the imagery in which the prophecy is framed, one cannot fail to understand the meaning of this, the greatest phase of the entire Odyssean journey. We are all free to decode and interpret the image within the limits of our own capacity not only to understand but to live. And here, in parentheses, one must hasten to add that one's capacity to understand never exceeds one's potential for living out what is fully understood. As always, the new meaning to come has to be acted out before it can be known, and no doubt, therefore, the imagery which confronts every imagination now that the imperviousness of the past millennia has been exposed, presents the inescapable challenge and charge from life itself to go forth with Odysseus.

On the face of it, it would seem a nonsense that he should set out for the mainland on a journey deep into its unknown heart carrying his finest cut ship's oar on his shoulder. Yet in its symbolic context the image is of great significance.

36

The oar is to the ship what the feather is to a bird; indeed this simile, which I thought came to me of its own natural accord, I find, on checking the original, is exactly the one used by Teiresias in Hades, so there can be no misunderstanding. The oar is the plenipotentiary in the imagination of all that the ship and the journey by sea, in Odysseus's painted ships with their crimson cheeks, have brought not only to Odysseus but to the human being in its exploration of the unknown world of his deepest self. It is the heraldic badge of all that his spirit has acquired in that long, searching encounter with the dark forces of the collective unconscious of man. It is the only appropriate emblem of his increased stature and awareness, and he does not so much carry it on his shoulder as wear it proudly, just as the ancient kings in Africa wore a feather of the sacred ibis, black and white, stuck into a metal halo around their head as a sign of royalty inspired by ultimate wisdom within.

With this conspicuously incongruous burden on his shoulder, Odysseus penetrates deep into the mainland – which serves as another form of 'the main' to which Donne referred. The fact that the image of the main which has to be joined is now no longer the deep sea but a vast, unknown land suggests what an enormous advance of the unconscious into consciousness has taken place since Odysseus left his plough in Ithaca to go, reluctantly, to war on the great plain of Troy. His feet are now clearly set on a new way, and his attitude to life before him is now on firm ground and no longer balancing on the boards of a heaving ship. He walks with firm and purposeful tread into the undiscovered land, so unknown and remote a country that its people, according to Teiresias, had never heard of the sea and did not even know the use of salt. This last reference to a people who do not know the use of salt is of immense meaning. Salt is of such importance to the wholeness and sanity of the human body that it is a unique image of the element of meaning and its role in the wholeness of the human spirit. The ancient world was fully aware of its alchemical significance, so that no one is in doubt about what Christ meant in the New Testament when he asked the question: 'And when the salt loses its savour, wherewith will you put it back again?' The thought of losing that savour, without any need of explanation, arouses an instinctive alarm that sends a shiver as of an acute ague in the spirit of all who hear it. So it is important not to forget this element of the journey as one penetrates deeply into the main with Odysseus, because it suggests why his mission cannot fail: the main needs, as a body needs, salt, needs the knowledge and realization of what the sea represents, and what he has to bring it of the individual experience of increasing the range of consciousness in the great collective unconscious of life. As so often in life, when all the resources of the conscious spirit fail and disaster threatens, the spirit concerned does not fail because, feeble as flesh and blood may be, it musters the strength needed in this correspondence of heart and mind to a fundamental necessity of life which cannot allow it to fail.

He travels thus until there comes a day when he meets a lone wayfarer, and the wayfarer asks him: 'What are you doing with that winnowing shovel on your shoulder?' One knows from illustrations that have come down to us from the past that Greek oars had a finely cut and scooped blade which closely resembled a shovel.

For me, as with so many of the images in Homer, the image was instantly conclusive because I knew the shape well. We still threshed our corn in my Africa not with machines as today but on threshing floors, with the sheaves of corn stacked out in circles, the ears of corn pointing to the centre of the enclosure, and a troop of horses was driven in to trample the sheaves under their hooves from morning till late afternoon. Then the straw would be pitched out and what was left underneath brushed with brooms into a vast pile of golden chaff, with even more golden grain showing through the torn and battered husks. We would then use not metal shovels, because they were too sharp and harsh and would damage the indispensable grain, but softer wooden shovels and fill them to the brim with corn and toss the contents high into the air, and as it all came down the air would sift the chaff from the corn. The process would be continued until, with all the chaff gone, only a beautiful symmetrical mountain of corn was left, to be joined in the days that followed by more and more corn garnered in this way until one had enough food to see one through the months, and if necessary even years, to come.

So this recognition symbolically is of the utmost significance. The moment of the harvest of all that Odysseus's spirit had earned had come; the moment when all that had been wrong and inadequate in his life before was to be transformed into food for survival and increase of an unknown new people, which is the most telling image of the vast unknown area of being and becoming in man still to be realized and, in its turn and measure, transcended.

So there, again as the prophecy demanded, he plants the oar deep as if it were a sapling of the tree of life itself that would grow high into the sky and stretch out its branches far and wide. Obviously, visually, the externals of Odysseus's mission and its consequences for the life of the future can be taken no further there. Yet the transplanted oar stands fast in the spirit of man to mark the place and the time and season when a great harvest in the life of all generations has to be gathered, when what is full of meaning is separated at last from what is meaningless, the real from the unreal, the truth from the error, and all is now seed for a vast enlargement of consciousness, and life is carried closer to the totality of creation, which is its purpose.

There remains only the last part of the prophecy and that, inevitably, is deeply concerned with the matter of sacrifice, sacrifice as an instrument of a law of creation that life does not move on until, where it has been impeded and blurred and marred by human error, that error has been corrected or – to use the word which conveys best the profound and solemn dimension of the spirit from which the need arises – redeemed. Odysseus's world had a wonderful blanket word which seems to cover all areas of human folly, error and misdirection. It is the word 'hubris', with its sense that whatever goes wrong in the life not only of men but even of gods and creation comes from excess, from the breach of proportion to which all that is lawful and ordered and creative in the universe is utterly, irrevocably bound and committed. It is only when the life that has succumbed to hubris has recognized the excess, not only consciously but fully in heart and mind, with an emotion of horror that can no longer be suppressed, in other words, when the spirit of the afflicted in this moment of recognition repents and so makes its peace again with the whole of life, that it is free to become part once again of the great sweep of its movement towards the future.

I refer deliberately to this sweep and movement because always, when the moment of reckoning with hubris comes, it follows a period in which life seems to have come to a halt, when it neither regresses nor progresses and time itself stands still. That is perhaps the greatest horror of it all; that is the moment when one realizes that hell and the ultimately unbearable suffering it symbolizes belongs to an area of the spirit where there is no time, no movement, no swing of the seasons in command of the seas and the land.

Even when the standstill is of the most enchanted and perfect and cushioned kind, as it was on Calypso's island where Odysseus himself was promised immortality and everlasting bliss with the loveliest of divine nymphs, bliss forever, he discovered, was a torment, and he longed for nothing more than to return to Penelope and the son he had left as a little boy and the wear and tear and ultimate mortality of an island prince.

The greatest illustration of all, perhaps, of the horror to life when it is deprived of its movement and its rhythm and therefore its seasons, is when it occurs in man's relationship with the gods, the greatest symbols of his creation, who are the source of his greatest meaning. When these are based on an absolute assumption that his gods are immortal and unchanging and condemned to repeat endlessly the patterns without change wherewith the human spirit and imagination had originally invested them, man's sense and power of increase and renewal diminish until all just stand still and, if not redeemed, die away, and the cultures once based on them so securely fall away and perish. Thus it was only through the appearance of Prometheus on the scene, and the god-like centaur Chiron, that these concepts and relationships in the classical world were able to break out of the paralysis of immortality and enter the awesome continuum of space and time in which the unfolding of creation went on and they too could come to terms with divine excess and distortion through re-enlistment in the great pattern of procreation, death and resurrection, and so carry the burden of all the four seasons which they had presupposed for the rest of creation.

So often, as in the Greek tragedies when the human spirit fails to deal with its own excesses, fate does it for them, as it does for instance again and again in *The Eumenides*, so that man can see himself as in a mirror and realize that what he inflicted on others by force is inflicted on himself and can only be averted by being freely and consciously transformed within himself. Inevitably, therefore, this last phase of the journey prescribed for Odysseus by the gods, if it is to have lasting meaning, has to end in redemption through sacrifice, above all sacrifice to Poseidon, who personifies in Greek mythology the power of whatever it is that rules as a master pattern of the great collective unconscious. Odysseus's greatest offences, even at the moment in life when his experience on the plains of Troy and after should have taught him to know better, had come out of an excess of the essential male qualities which he had inherited in such a great abundance and inspired way. Both his instinctive and his actual life had compelled him to spend so much of his doing in use of these qualities that he had ceased to be their master and become their indulgent servant. They are represented here in the heart of the unknown continent where he has planted his oar and gathered his final harvest, by a bull, a ram and a breeding boar.

The bull and the ram are perhaps the aspects most accessible to his consciousness. The bull represents always the excess of masculine power and glory in both gods and men in all the immense stride of the years in which the masculine powers have usurped and dominated all other aspects of life and the spirit, particularly the feeling and the caring and what were to become the Eros aspects of life, which even the great services that masculine power rendered the feminine in the battle for survival could not justify or redeem. The ram represents the collective masculine, because there is no animal image to be found which is so utterly dedicated to the collective values and their uses as the sheep. And the hubris of the ram is that he would confine the values of the collective exclusively to an endless process of procreation and recreation of the species, making 'sheep in sheep's clothing' of a humanity imprisoned in the unrelenting repetition of the pattern which evoked in T. S. Eliot, after his experience of the wasteland in his spirit and the hollowness in men, the despairing utterance: 'birth, and copulation, and death, that's all the facts, when you come down to brass tacks'. It is not for nothing that the vision of the value of the collective and its power in *The Odyssey* is in the Cyclops, Polyphemus, the one-eyed tyrant whose power is dedicated entirely to the welfare of the sheep. Confronted with this power which would destroy Odysseus and his men, Odysseus with his two-eyed vision outwits the tyrant but, in the moment of his triumph, exceeds the proportion which has all along been demanded of him in the lust he has acquired for battle in the war against Troy. He is seduced into self-aggrandizement, boasting and gloating. The compassion that had always been potential in lawful battle and killing was denied to him, and his behaviour against the proportions became so outrageous that the blinded Titan nearly destroyed him and his crew by hurling rocks after him, and the Titan's father, Poseidon, was so outraged by this egotistical male excess that he became full of vengeance in his turn and the embittered persecutor of Odysseus, nearly wrecking his great quest on many occasions before he was allowed by the gods to come home to Ithaca.

And finally there is perhaps the most dangerous of all the masculine personifications, the breeding boar, the masculine in its most natural, its wildest abundance and most undifferentiated state. Although the source of great energies in the spirit of man, it is also a source of corruption by sheer power because of its ignorance of the fateful law of proportion and lack of consciousness. Between them the bull, the ram and the breeding boar are dynamic images of the whole range of the sources of the masculine excesses by

43

which Odysseus had been repeatedly and almost lethally tempted because of being momentarily seduced by them in his life. However, here in this great continent, in the heart of the vast unknown main, Odysseus is at the place in the centre of himself where the mystery of redemption and recommitment of the totality of himself to life, as in a eucharist in a holy of holies of the universe, is about to take place and through the relevant sacrifice renew spirit and being in the winter of life. If he fails in this, he fails in all else, and his odyssey might as well not have been.

Here Helen Luke introduces a nuance of her own which does not diminish the meaning of the prophecy but adds to it. She is far too loyal to both the spirit and the letter of the Teiresian prescription to violate it, but her true feminine intuition brings out what is implicit in the unfolding of the imagery without having been made specific by the blind seer. She knows that this moment of sacrifice would not have been happening if it had not been for the reawakening and enlargement of the new relationship Odysseus had acquired with his feminine element, and she brings it out most delicately and conclusively in the way Odysseus sets out to find the breeding boar for the sacrifice.

Obviously he would have had no difficulty in procuring the bull and the ram he needed from the people of the wayfarer, but a breeding boar, the most dangerous of them all, wild, fierce, unpredictable and uncompromised by any regular association with man except as an enemy to be mercilessly hunted down and killed, is another matter. This final and most dangerous phase of his reckoning with the gods has to be faced by him, alone as he has never been on his pilgrimage, in this dark forest at the heart of the unknown main. He has no arms of any kind and knows that the wayfarer can be of no further help to him. Appalled inwardly, he has to summon up all that he has of courage

44

in his great spirit and set forth with outwardly only a rope formed into a noose in his hands. Yet within, he has something he never had before. It is something implicit in the prophecy which Helen Luke makes specific and explicit: she sees him armed now with something essentially of the feminine Penelope has brought alive within him, feelings of care and sympathy for all that lives and breathes which are born in the heart of every women as her portion of the role of the Great Mother life needs for its survival and fulfilment. She sends him forth with a prayer on his lips and with a song, born of the power and glory of the harmony of the masculine and feminine and the oneness of their diversities, already forming deep within his spirit. No longer are the gods presiding over this critical part of his life uncalled, as they have so often been. In this final crisis of his journey they are, as the image of prayer tells us, called to be at his side.

Before long he hears the boar pushing through the brush and wood with great energy and obviously already his full, aggressive self. She makes Odysseus step aside onto a flat rock, an image of the firm foundation on which the new awareness has been laid, as if to let the boar pass, if its impetuous nature demands it. But at that moment the song of harmony and order, the song that might have come from Apollo, the god of music himself, breaks out of him. Amazed, he hears himself singing; and as he sings, the music, as always when it is not only heard but being made as well, has the power of enabling the human being to become the order and the ultimate harmony which it serves and, while the music lasts, to make all that has the sense to hear around him become part of that order and harmony as well.

The boar, who has never encountered man except as an enemy before, and whose first experience therefore this is

45

of the harmony and illumination which accompanies the music, is instantly gripped and totally within its power. It is to me a sort of early *Tempest* moment: it is kin in its instinctual way to the moment when Caliban, who on that island full of strange noises has intrigued so hard and diligently with the conspirators to murder his master, sees Prospero finally in a new transfigured way, when all that is negative is abolished and all that has been excessive and hurtful in the past is forgiven. As Prospero is about to proclaim to the world, while pointing at Caliban, '. . . this thing of darkness I acknowledge mine', Caliban, seeing Prospero for what he truly is, exclaims: 'How fine my master is!'

All resolution of opposites in life, of course, implies a transcendence of paradox; and perhaps the greatest form of transcendence made manifest in creation is the transcendence that is also a synchronicity of extremes, of that which has appeared throughout life as if all would always be contradiction, always holding one another at infinite arms length in a strange love-hate polarity. But ultimately, in a moment when a wholeness of spirit is at last attained, the two extremes of the human spirit suddenly embrace. These things perhaps come from what could be an as yet unacknowledged and unexplored probability that life and creation are the greatest of all synchronicities of matter and spirit, and that what the seers and prophets call divine grace is the greatest among the great.

And here, in the heart of the main, it is as if the image of such a synchronicity of boar and man alone can complete the sum of the sacrifice. The boar, which represents the deepest and most archaic dimension of the unconscious, and is a personification of the deepest male instinctual element in man at its least known and most dangerous condition, suddenly succumbs to the great overall longing in the unconscious for harmony and illumination, and claims his birthright in darkness to be kin and part of the wholeness which is Odysseus's ultimate mission. He comes quietly forward and stretches out his head so that Odysseus can put the noose around his neck, tighten it gently, and then the two of them turn about and he goes almost willingly, in a way that brings tears to Homer's listeners, to the place of sacrifice, the place that an old Zulu oral historian, describing an ancient rite of sacrifice to me, called: 'The place where one goes to be known at last, as the first spirit has all along known one.'

All this has taken great courage, not only on the part of Odysseus but also those who have amplified the story, because the more one recognizes the image and follows the amplification of its meaning, the greater the ethical charge imposed on the human soul that, to the extent and measure whereto the image has become known, one is part of an extended universal obligation which never again can be disowned without serious consequences for the sanity and welfare of human consciousness. One has no option but to choose between living out the enlarged awareness fully, or evading it and seeing it diminish lethally as a result.

This emphasis, even at the risk of being repetitive, is today more than ever necessary because the hubris of reason and its 'isms' which dominate the intellectual day would undoubtedly regard such a statement as an irrelevant indulgence of fantasy, but it would be even poorer for it than it already is. For reason itself is rooted in these ancient images in which the Teiresian prophecy is expressed and demands more than a literal reading before it will surrender the immense wealth of primordial insights and experiences of life which are held in the deep of the unconscious to those who have the courage to follow to their true end all the implications that arise in the process of amplification, the hints of new possibilities of being and meaning, and at times what appear to the sheer mind as trivial and the most palpable impossibilities. Indeed, again and again what is capable of the greatest meaning is presented to the over-rational mind as most trivial and insignificant. So it has been in the first of the myths, the legends and the stories and, ultimately, more and more as one's life draws to its own apparent close, the dreams of mankind, and one has no doubt at all therefore that what is so sensitively and lovingly amplified, as it is in the Helen Luke version, is an authentic part of the Odyssean pattern in us all.

Odysseus is free then to return to Ithaca and there to discharge the last of the tasks laid upon him in Hades. Great as is Poseidon, the brother of Zeus, to whom he has already performed sacrifices in the heart of the main, these are not enough. He still has to perform sacrifices to each and every one of the gods in their just order for what is valid and proportionate, however small or infinitesimal, in each of them. He has to emancipate himself from any tend-ency, however slight it may have been, to seek favours from any particular god. It is a sign that his spirit is now fully aware that the human being should no longer seek special dispensation for himself from any of the gods, because favours and special divine patronage have become archaic, and in the Odyssean past these favours, conferred by indi-vidual gods without reference to the whole, were only ever ambivalent gifts and the sources also of envies and jealous-ies, both in heaven and earth, inevitably dividing one man against another, groups of men against one another, and even plunging the gods on Olympus into strife and horren-dous rivalries, so that the thunder and lightning of Zeus as made manifest in Ithaca has always to be thrown at the trespassers of the law, even when the trespasser is a goddess and daughter of the greatest god of all, to bring god and men back within the law of harmony and order.

It was only when all these sacrifices, from the greatest to the smallest, have been made that the great prophecy is fulfilled and Odysseus himself is able to lead what is left of his life with a wisdom which at last could grow and be dedicated without distortion or impediments within, so that Odysseus's journey in the here and now could end in the gentlest of deaths that would come to him like a mist out of the sea.

With this second and final return of Odysseus to Ithaca, not only is it the end of the Odyssean pattern in every man, it seems as if one is abandoned totally in what is left of life without the guidance which this mythmaking, this story-telling thing in life had so mysteriously given.

In my own case I have tried to follow it out in what is written here, and in the chapters to come, from the experience of a 'Once upon a time . . .' face and the first revelation in my life of the divine imperative when thunder and lightning flashed and spoke in a voice that made a drum of the earth, and an antique voice of a man of a vanished race called on his God and told his companions that they had to listen, because the God was speaking.

From that first moment I have tried always to listen in a way which, without my knowing, also became a journey of exploration of a vast new universe within myself; and no matter how confused and troubled, or how destructive and apparently lethal at times the circumstances of my life, this mythmaking, storytelling thing in mankind has always been a kind of golden thread out of the labyrinth which has been the life of my time. And this sense of being utterly and forever reclaimed by an island self at times induced in me a helplessness and emptiness such as I had never experienced, and I was tempted to think that the myth of my own life was failing me, not because it was false or inadequate in itself but because it was perhaps the prelude to a greater myth somewhere of which I did not know. But even if it was, how could I measure one myth against another and say that this is more meaningful, and that one there is greater? How, when the myth arises in the area where meaning rules and is the only measure, can anyone say that there is one greater than another? I myself, confined as I am utterly in the relativity of reality which carries the label, however provisionally, of a space/time continuum and its expanding universe, could only cling to the fact, as Odysseus clung to the first rock in Nausicaa's island when he was about to be delivered from his trials, that I find myself securely rooted and standing in this myth because it was with me in the beginning, never ceased to grow, and is with me still.

Meanwhile there are many other myths to which the human spirit owes almost as much, if not, in their sum, more. And yet closely related to the Homeric theme as they might be, it still remains a dominant because it serves so precisely a pattern which is in every man and woman, a pattern which is both a first and a last, and which contains the human being from his awakening in the birth which, as the Wordsworthian quotation earlier on had it, was a kind of sleeping, on to where he re-enters the dimension wherein his life star arose. And there, in his own 'now', to the extent to which the journey presupposed has been travelled to its true end where all the gods and men are at one at last, being becomes part of what will, to the generations of another future, be a 'Once upon a time . . .' All that was false and redundant stripped and fallen away, as it is symbolized at the place of sacrifice in the main and its pagan 'holy of holies', the 'I' and 'thou' at one, man shall know at last as he all along has been known.

All this would seem to imply that the Odyssean myth is the final myth and there is no more to come. But this is not so. It is true only about this journey from the 'Once upon a time . . .' world towards the great 'Once upon a time . . .' to come. Neither it nor the little memory and the great memory which have conducted us so faithfully seem to take us any further. Their role moreover for the moment is abolished in a present when man has decided not only to forget his past but with a strange, bright-eyed wilfulness conducts himself as if the past has never been and he can make the future without any need of it himself; that indeed he can make the future as if the past were perhaps an irrelevance, if not the greatest hindrance, to his task. He is gripped by a strange compulsion and, by use of his own rational faculties for purposes for which they were not intended, into a delusion that he could make it all new and better by himself for people like himself. As a result, his contact with the image-making part of himself, with the imagination as a whole in the sense that Blake used it and where the myths that have always informed man of a deeper and a greater self arise, has been so diminished as to be almost nonexistent.

It is shown so clearly in the language he uses today and in what he writes with such a marked and strained rational obsession with that which is external, visible and felt through the senses and, at best, weighed in instruments of his own design. His vocabulary in this regard is increasingly dessicated and deprived of colour; and something, for which one can only use the antique word 'magic', that was invested in the living word when it first burst like a star in the night into the consciousness of the first man, has vanished from his thought.

The magic of the living word, which depends on its closeness to the image that gave it birth, and the distance which the person who uses the word today has put between himself and that moment are there for all to see; one has only to look up any of the words in most common use in the dictionary and see how far it has travelled from what it meant at its origin. Every word in the beginning was wisely provided for by life to sustain something of its own which the person who used it could only destroy by putting the word to slanted and partial uses. However, it was never intended that words were to be imprisoned in their first, immediate use, because part of this magic was that every word was a seed, and, with its fellow seeds, all could be sown in their season like corn in a ploughed field and would grow together into a new awareness, accessible to the mind of man. What has happened today, though, is not a growth of the word rooted in its image but a violation and a cutting-away of the roots, so that the word becomes like the seed in the parable that fell by the wayside. How far, for instance, has the modern mind travelled that it could corrupt so lovely a word as 'gay' and contract it to so pointed and specialized a use as it has today? How far has one not gone, and how much is there not to relearn, when one travels the whole distance of what separates the original 'merci' from its corporate role in what we call 'com*merce*' today?

There are innumerable examples of the difference between what was once the living word and the lame, convoluted language the television man of today talks to his kind. One can orchestrate this impoverishment in the decline of fantasy in human intercourse and communication, the decline of the story, and the surrogate, dreary realism that has taken its place. But it ought not to be necessary to belabour the theme, so obvious and widespread is this devaluing of the word into presenters' 'televese'.

This decline of the living word is not a recent phenomenon. It has happened in many other cultures before, and at the beginning of the nineteenth century, after two centuries of rationalism, it was intrinsic in all that Blake had to say about art when he warned how nations decay when the arts decay. The threat was already there in the world that was rooted firmly, it seemed for ever, in the mythmaking spirit out of which *The Odyssey* and the great tragedies, poetry and arts of Greece arose, almost fountain-wise, and even the axioms, hypotheses and concepts of science spouted up most unscientifically to become the spirit and exercise of the science we know today. At this moment of return to Ithaca, though, the great epics were not written or read out aloud but were alive, without written shapes to enclose them as in straitjackets of the letters, and still issuing warm and full of the magic of their birth straight from the lips of living men to the listening ears and minds, hungry and eager to receive them, not just for the use of the moment but for what they brought with them of their own accord, free of charge as it were, from the birth of consciousness and its orchestrations in the imperative imagination of mankind, anticipating and perhaps even justifying Wordsworth's grand description of the soul of man born 'trailing clouds of glory from God, who is our home'.

Yet that world which, in hindsight, seemed so secure in its natural roots that reached far down into the image-making imagination was in its turn to be threatened, among other correlated factors, by the increase of the contrived and artificial word, aided and abetted by the bias of writing and the increased availability of books. It is not surprising that the greatest philosophers, like Aristotle and Socrates, would not resort to writing because, great an invention as it was, it exposed the word to a kind of betrayal in which the pen and the rationalism of the day gave an undue role to calculation, deliberation and all the many adjectives which contribute to an exercise of the rational hubris in the intellectually ambitious fashion of the day, and obeisance to the power as opposed to the feeling and immediacy of the word. Looking back over the age which separates us today from Socrates, it is not hard to see why, when he was asked what had gone wrong with the spirit of Greece, he said, only a few hours before he took hemlock, it was all due to the fact that there were too many books in Greece.

This, of course, is not in any way an attack on reason but only on the 'isms' that men made of reason. Reason, within lawful proportion, is a quintessential ingredient of wholeness, and the most significant example of what I mean comes from the great and most inspired master of reason, Aristotle. Like Socrates, he never wrote but entrusted all that he had to say to the living word, usually delivered walking up and down with listeners anxious to hear his spontaneous message, as if in the walking too he was emphasising that the living word was designated for men of spirit, and minds always on a journey. How Socrates would have summed it all up ultimately if his life had not been cut short by his sentence to death we can never know, but we can know enough from the impact he had on Plato on what a momentous journey his living words took the spirit of his day.

Also one does know that the happier placed Aristotle, as the moment came when he had served, as I believe he had to the full, both the little and the great memory and the story of himself, and drew nearer to the fulfilment of his own myth, this greatest of all Plato's pupils declared: 'A friend of wisdom is also a friend of the myth'. Then in a letter to an intimate friend not long before his death he confessed: 'The lonelier I am, the more of a recluse I become, the greater is my love for myths'.

Today we know well enough what happened to the

Greeks when they lost their mythological, image-making contact with life. We know only too well also how the Roman contribution to life, great as it was, was impeded and ultimately doomed to decline because of the absence of the living myth and its substitution in something called 'mythology'.

Finally, in our own Christian world there is the redeeming example of Christ who, likewise, even though one knows that he was a great scholar, entrusted the whole of his message to the living word. And again one can measure what is almost the greatest of all wastelands in between the magical word, the alchemical transforming word of the parables, and what dogma and exegesis of the Bible and theology have made of them.

As for myself, my own record of the role of the little and the great memory in my life shows how the most ancient of stone-age societies to which we still had access in my youth stayed integrated when it was rooted in its own myths, legends and stories, in contrast to the disintegration that has followed almost everywhere in the great primitive societies of Africa when they lost their story, and junior lecturers from the proliferating universities in Europe took over from witchdoctors and seers and prophets, with their own rational and moth-eaten ideologies that could not be honourably lived. Having known that world well, I can only testify how, in what I have called my own effort at listening to the thunder, I was often reading and listening in company of the memory I had of Greeks and Trojans and the mythological patterns with which I had become familiar. I would notice, for instance, how even before Homer composed his great epic songs of *The Iliad* and *The Odyssey*, the courts of the Greek princes great and small were constantly visited by singers and minstrels singing what they called 'the praise of the deeds of gods and heroes'.

55

I would remember this as I heard Zulu and Xhosa and
'Tswana chiefs repeat to me what they called the 'praise
names' of the heroes of the past, until there came a day
when at the age of eighteen I went to visit a new prophet
who had arisen among the Zulus, one of the most beautiful
men in spirit and mind and body I have ever met, and he
asked me why I had come to see him. And I told him I had
come because I thought he could tell me more about the
Great First Spirit, Umkulunkulu, than the men I met in
cities could tell me. Sadly he shook his head and said to
me: 'Men no longer speak of Umkulunkulu. His praise
names are forgotten and they speak only of things that are
useful to them.' And after a long pause he added: 'Men do
not die when they die. They only die when their praise
names are forgotten, and then we die with them.'

So in these Bushman and early Bantu societies I knew as
a boy, the main instrument of a sense of religion, and of
art which arises in the same dimension of our spirit,
expressed itself almost totally in the living word and the
wonderful gift they had of using it in all its immediacy. It
went even deeper, for it was more primitive at the moment
of my early contact, than it did as far as I knew in the pre-
Homeric phase of Greek civilization. It was not only used
in connection with their Great First Spirit for the dialogue
between God and man, and their remembrance of the past
in the sense that everything in their life was myth, legend
and story and above all the story of life and man rooted in
their soul and its own perceptions, but also it provided
them with a sense of wonder. It provided them with a sense
of the living mystery of life, and as a result it helped to
heighten their sensitivities, their own perceptions and ultimately their total awareness. It carried them on and gave
them a sense of continuation which all the millennia of their

wandering through the darkness of the darkest continent on earth could not quench.

So it was as if with this too they were on a journey in time and space with life and creation and always travelling on, with this praise-name pattern as their container, and with it a profound instinctive reverence for all forms of life; a form of reverence which expressed itself also in an unquestioned obligation to show as much respect to the phenomena and creatures of nature as they did to one another and to their Great First Spirit.

Dante, in his great epic of the soul, stresses how on the journey from the depths of hell to the heights of heaven he became aware of how, the nearer he drew to Paradise the more courteous the spirits became to one another; the greater the grace, the sense of the ultimate, the more moving and transforming the courtesy of one form would be to another. And what was most striking to me in my contact with the antique and primitive forms of life in Africa was to see how great and universal was the courtesy, how immediate and binding the instinctive politeness – as our own, increasingly discarded and shallow word for courtesy would have it. For instance, one of their most common forms of greeting of even a stranger seen at a distance was: 'I see you. Yes, I see you.'

And the stranger likewise would reply: 'Yes. I see you too.'

And from the tone, and the great salute of the right hand raised that went with it, one realized that it was not just a seeing with the eyes but a way of recognizing the common humanity and its living bonds they all shared.

I would think of the streets of London and the capitals of the world, of people all day walking past one another and not only not seeing one another in this way but walking

57

past as if all in the streets were there only as an impediment to their own going.

Moreover, the obligation which this awakening of courtesy imposed upon their behaviour influenced their attitude to natural phenomena. For instance, these people of the living language, when asked the way by a stranger like myself, if it happened that they had to point to the north-west, the quarter whence their rains would come, would consider it rude to point an index finger in that direction and make the offended rain perhaps delay its coming, so out of courtesy they would do the necessary pointing knuckle-first, with the finger doubled back.

But the most moving example in my own experience of how deep and essential a part this was of the climate of grace and resolution in the human spirit was an encounter I shared once with an old Zulu guide who was one of the great men of Africa, in my own measure of greatness. It happened on an early summer's afternoon in the bush of northern Zululand. We had paused for a much-needed rest in the shade of a great sycamore fig tree. Suddenly one of the most magical birds I know, a honey-guide, appeared and perched on a bush nearby and immediately set up an imperious song, commanding us to be up and to follow it. Most of us, particularly those who had an experience of the honey-guide and knew on what a long journey it could take one to where it had discovered its nest of honey, were very tired and determined that our rest was more important than the honey-guide's desires. And although the honey-guide's chatter was becoming more angry and therefore less harmonious, and to tired spirits more irritating, this old Zulu, shaming men half his age who preferred their ease to answering the call of a mere bird, got to his feet and began to chant to the bird in a voice with tones and an expression on his face as if we were in some kind of wayside chapel rather than stretched out in the glimmering bush. One man, who was very close to the old Zulu, and I myself felt compelled to get to our feet and join him as the bird took off from the bush. The old man followed after it, without ceasing to chant. He was chanting in what my friend, who knew Zulu well, called 'Shakespearean Zulu', and he was chanting a song composed almost entirely of the praise names of the bird, and a long record of all the sweetness and delight he had brought to men in removing bitterness not only from their tongues but from their hearts and minds and lives as well. As we went, the honey-guide's irritation left its voice and it went ahead in short laps of flight from one prominent bush to another, so that it could check at a glance that we were following. It went on until evening when we came to the nest and, alas, found it empty. The honey-guide's voice declined into a pitiful little gurgle and then was silent. And in that long light of an African evening drawing to a close in the bush, it ultimately took off and vanished. But our Zulu guide went on for a while with his chanting, producing more praise and grace of a formal and melodious farewell which, with all that had happened, combined in a wondrous way to turn what had been on one level a defeat of our little mission into a triumph of partnership between man and bird, demonstrating also how it was transparent with the spirit of Eros of which the bee, its honey and the great service it renders procreation of the plants by pollenizing the flowers that come with the rain, lives on in the imagination of Africa as one of the greatest symbols of love in action. The First Spirit of the Bushmen, for instance, is said, after his theft of fire from the ostrich, to have put on all the different colours of the animals and the birds and their eggs with honey, as a mark of the sweetness that is the love of his all-embracing disposition.

When we came back to camp, one of those who had

stayed behind and was rather a know-all said: 'I knew all along it was foolish to expect to find any honey at this time of year in this part of the bush, otherwise I might have come with you.'

His tone made the drift of what he had said so clear that, although our old guide did not speak English, he was aroused into a rebuke not only of the man but almost of the whole world which we represented. Again, in that Shakespearean Zulu of his, with a voice to match it, he said: 'It is more important to be with the honey-bird when he fails to find the honey – because that will show him one is really his friend – than it would be only to go with him when he finds lots of honey, because if we only go then he will know that we do not go with him as a friend but with only greed in our hearts.'

With all this, however, I do not mean to give the impression of an attack on the written word, to which life owes so much, above all in the quintessential part it has played in promoting and enlarging the area of remembrance which is essential for the continuity and promotion of all forms of life, but merely to emphasize again what seems utterly lost in the values of man, that the written language languishes and becomes dispirited if it loses its interdependence and closeness to the language of the living and immediate word as well as the imagery out of which it arises. Whenever I have thought of my experience of a culture rooted in the living word, I recall the honey-guide, and the many other orchestrations of the reverence for life of which it was the principal expression, and I am amazed how examples from other even more conscious and sophisticated cultures confirm the extent of the wide dominion of the word that was in the beginning.

And here I think of the great chapter in St John where Christ tells his disciples that he will have to leave them, implying almost that if he stayed his great example could be a hindrance to them in their lesser capacities of spirit. But seeing their distress he tells them he will leave behind a guide that could not fail them; and that is what the Christian world to this day calls the Holy Spirit. But under whatever name it is designated in other religions and cultures, it is always as the sacred source from which all love and knowledge of the truth comes. And one thinks inevitably of its pentecostal manifestation and bequest to the bereft apostles which, hard upon the appearance of the tongues of fire, its strange gift of tongues brought alive in all of them so that they could talk, unlettered and unready as they were, to every one of the multitudes of creeds and colours and races in that far-flung outpost of the mighty Roman Empire and immediately be understood; and the message that the words conveyed began to spread like those fires started by lightning in dry grass and bush, and spread far and wide to inflame ultimately also the rulers of one of the greatest empires the world has ever seen.

Yet what I have had to offer and in what follows, long as it may seem, is but a brief summary of the role in my own life of myths and legends and stories rooted in the living word and its natural imagery. In so far as there is any merit in what I am trying to say, and even in what I do, it has depended a great deal on what I have come to call the climate of the human spirit and soul. Just as the best the Christian myth can do for a description of the creator is 'that which cannot be named', something of which there is a natural commandment not even to have specific images, it is a something I can neither define nor conceptualize. Yet it is perhaps the most important of all dimensions in human awareness. In so far as the word lives and the images form and come and go and the symbols shine in the darkness of our great unknowing to inform us of possibilities of life and meaning, they do so in a state of utter dependence and interdependence with this climate. It is almost as if there were an ecology of meaning within us, an environment of the soul and the spirit as crucial for the wellbeing, the growth and the vigour of all the ideas, perceptions, forms of beauty and visions of the future and the infinite diversity of great imponderables and options which are its forms of life, and as dependent upon it and its season as those of the world without.

It is not just an idle analogy, an orchestration of pathetic fallacies, for as I have grown older there seems to me a mysterious bond, a vital and infinite closeness of inter-relationship between the invisible world, this great inner objectivity we experience subjectively within, and the great objective world and its universe without. The wellbeing of both these, I have come to believe, is indivisible, and this label of 'fantasy' with which the rationalists reject this life-giving parallelism of climates and ecologies can no longer stick and misdirect the reawakening awareness that the human being cannot be creative and maintain the sanity and wholeness of one without the other. Men just cannot do to this world within what they do not also do to the world without, and to the world without, that which does not provoke a corresponding consequence within. These worlds, which we are contracted by life to experience where they meet in us so subjectively and are compelled at the centre of ourselves to commit the whole of our ration of life on earth to the welfare of both, seem increasingly so close as if they were perhaps a transcendent form of the greatest manifestation conceivable which can be registered in human senses and imagination – what physicists and psychologists today combine to call the phenomenon of 'synchronicity'.

Ever since I had more time to myself than I would have

had in a normal life, in periods of solitary confinement in prisons during the war, the thought has assailed me: perhaps all is synchronicity? As I have thought of the natural images I have served in primitive and civilized environments, an overwhelming feeling has come to me that there is in the world around us not a form of life, not a stone, not a crystal, not a plant, not the smallest insect or the greatest beast that walks on the earth or swims in the ocean, not the moss which is perhaps the first and most moving image of the need of the organic for the inorganic in the life of plants and grass, conquering and clinging to the stone it has conquered, that is not synchronized in every detail and limited to an equal something within; and that life and creation in itself is the synchronicity, all paradox and polarity transcended in a great acausal moment with which creation as we know it began and moves on.

I say this with acute feelings of its approximation, but am compelled to say it nonetheless because it is as much as I can do. And the importance of realizing how this climate of the spirit is something which has always been there, demands it. It is possible that we ourselves can contribute positively to promoting this climate by being more and more aware of its needs as much as its uses, and being obedient particularly to the reverence and the wonder it inspires within our senses. But it is not of our making, and all that comes from it ultimately is known only through its affects in profound emotions and feelings that stir us of their own accord as in some synchronized vision in the external world. This can be illustrated not so much in words as through their happening. To take the commonest of examples, as the dawn, red in the morning, or the sunset in flames at night, stir their synchronised partner in the world within and confront the ego with their full synchronistic reality, they become mythological events of extreme and overwhelming significance, and the poor old ego, which for so long has thought of itself as author of all that there is in the human spirit of poetry, music, art, song, the praise and the story, is overwhelmed by so great a presumption and inclined to fall on its knees in an attitude of what it inadequately calls prayer, realizing the smallness of its role in these mythological matters, and realizing too that all such invention and creativity have come out of this double environment like birds winging out of the blue, particularly, as in my own case, like the honey-guide for our African selves to be set on a way of the spirit to the honey which is the ultimate symbol of Eros.

And yet, humbled as it may be for the sake of proportion and truth, it is upheld and glorified that, as the essential bearer of the message, fulfilling this part of its contract with life, it has become part of the message itself, and one feels that, even when it crumbles into dust, the essence of what has begun as a transient element is transformed into a truth which moves with creation. As an ancient African saying had it: 'The wood burns out but the fire burns on.' And it is the solace and the meaning of this wood to the flame of consciousness it has been, and without which consciousness could not have been, that it is forever part of the fire which will never burn out.

In some such way as this, by following the patterns of the great and the little memory, the myth, the legend, the story and the imagery of the first people of my part of Africa, as well as the people who have enriched culture and civilization and make us feel that even at this late hour the human spirit is redeemable and shall not be allowed to fail, I have found a meaning in life which I believe I could not have found in any other way. For me, as a result, it has become self-evident that the wounding of our great Mother Earth almost to death by our excesses and lack of love for what gave us birth has been accompanied by a similar decline of the healing power native to the world within and wounded to the same extent, and that if the one dies the other dies.

What then? The question fills me with greater dread than any question I have asked before, because – although in my own life I have on several occasions been through moments which seemed my last, and these moments have never lost their tendency to recall themselves from time to time, accompanied by feelings of a fear which my protective self did not allow me to feel at the time because they would have hindered my chances of survival – the answer now concerns not just the fate of oneself but of all life and all living things in a way they have not been threatened, I believe, since the moss first found life and in desperation clung to the inorganic stone for survival and continuation. And yet, even at this late hour, there is still enough left of the great climate in the spirit, and the climate in the world without, that in this area from which the little memory and the great memory, the myths and the legends and the living words all arise, there is a 'something else' which can redeem it. It is something to which Shakespeare, in one of his most memorable sonnets, refers as 'the prophetic soul of the wide world dreaming on things to come'.

In this reference to the prophetic soul of the world, dreaming of things to come, one finds the hope which lies imperishable and undiminished at the bottom of the Pandora's box of our time. It helps too towards an understanding of why Homer left the ultimate journey of Odysseus embedded in a prophetic state in his story. The dreaming prophetic state of our awareness is pregnant always with what is beyond our 'now', and this axiomatic truth in particular has the profound implication of where the human being has to turn for help when he finds himself not only at the end of his specific mythological journey and his own equivalent of reunion in Ithaca, but where he has to turn for guidance of his individual self in the future. Lost as his spirit may be, and suddenly as it seems without a myth and without its supporting legends, stories and the thousand-and-one implications and intimations of direction in art, literature and song, and the social institutions designed to support him in this predicament, bankrupt, empty and distressed, it is as if he is in the kind of wasteland of which T. S. Eliot spoke, corresponding to a great desert plain in himself, like the vast area deep in the Kalahari Desert which the first people of the land referred to as 'the place where the heart cries out: Oh, mother! I am lost!'

This moment in the full synchronistic spirit of itself is made all the more desperate with the spectacle of a planet by the day more endangered, and all around itself it sees, with a paradoxical, unbelieving belief, what corresponds in every detail to the change of climate and the ecological desecration and devastation in the soul and spirit within. But however desperate and rapid the course of a two-dimensional stampede towards destruction now appears, there is profound hope in this reference to the prophetic element which is the real ending of *The Odyssey*. In symbols there that have never failed us in the past, there is hope and intimation of a way forward, as there was for Odysseus when he had fulfilled his duty as husband, father, and king in Ithaca, and for the first time in his life gone on the journey of his soul just for his soul's sake alone.

And, what is most important, one cannot regard this journey as something that was applicable to Odysseus alone, because the Odyssean pattern, we know now, is in the spirit of every man and woman. It is impossible to think and above all to believe that we can belong to all that has gone before, and yet not to what is beyond Ithaca.

Consciously or unconsciously, whether we like it or not, all that is valid in our past, all that has gone into the creation and making of life on earth, determines that we are not imprisoned in the past; and however we may have failed now, whether we know it or not, we are dynamically pledged to the resolution of our own Odyssean pattern by journeying on alone, individual, distinct and immediate, at last part of the greater community to come, no longer a vast undifferentiated social collectivity but a congregation, as Dante found in his Paradise, where he came to the inmost circle of the creator, heaven stacked all about him with soul upon soul who had made that journey from Inferno, Purgatory and on to arrive, as the poet says with a great lift of spirit, each individual soul itself and intact and yet at one with all.

So it is time to look again at the basic symbolism of *The Odyssey*, above all the symbolism which all myths and legends and stories present as a journey, a journey through night and day, a journey through time, a journey through great and unexplored wastelands, a journey out of a great garden in the beginning, and after many a summer a return to where we left it unconsciously, but then and now see for the first time. This journey of Odysseus, alone with his own soul, indeed introduces something new that is not in all the great mythological journeys which shine like beacons in the dark of the vanished cultures and civilizations behind us. Yet we know the symbolism only too well in its archaic terms in the way it has been interpreted and reinterpreted by some three thousand years of men and women who have lived it and been inspired by it and interpreted it as faithfully as they could in the terms of the idioms and contexts of their own days. These interpretations are valid only as material to build on. They are not there for an *encore* in the theatre of life, however enthusiastic the audiences who have lost the heart to move on. Repetition has but diminished their achievement, and when we put our hands to our hearts and say we no longer have a modern myth, the myths and the gods are dead, what we are really saying is that the established interpretations of the past have died. What we need is an interpretation which is valid and contemporary and part of this prophetic soul dreaming of things to come, with all its intimations of what has been, and what is now, still in place to support what is to come. Great as these illuminations of the interpretation of what is behind us have been, and inspired as one can be in the stillness of the dark of the imaginations of our day by the way they sweep the last horizons behind us as if they were lighthouses to guide the navigators of life over dangerously unknown oceans and, as they one by one sink behind us as we are compelled, Odysseus-like, to travel on alone, we have only one area of ourselves to turn to, to know how to steer: the dream that is wide and fast in the prophetic soul of every man.

Resetting our courses in this dreaming dimension where our symbols and images are woven, Penelope-like, into the pattern of the future which unravels itself at the end of every accomplished day lest it be an impediment to what is to come at dawn of the next, one is amazed how truly these lighthouses have performed their function in the spirit's navigation from the first moment to the present, and how fast these great imponderables will stand in preserving our continuity from the beginning to wherever it may want to end. The course we planned in the dark of our spirit for the future would have been incomplete without each one of them and their reference on the chart of life. The myth to come would in fact be hollow, as Eliot's hollow men were hollow, if they were not already part of the raw material of the future as a whole, and preparation for a fateful increase of human awareness.

But what is it that makes one feel certain that it is a point of renewal, and a prospect of a leap forward in the spirit of the life of man on earth? And in posing the question in terms of what is new and old, one must not forget for a moment the paradox of it all that the first becomes the last and the last becomes the first, and in a sense it is a point that life has often reached in the past, instinctively and intuitively, but could not carry on beyond, because it lacked this great 'something else'; it lacked the means of a kind of awareness which would enable man to carry on consciously from where he had arrived instinctively and intuitively. Man failed this opportunity of renewal which return to the point where he had started gave him, because the enlargement of consciousness to make it contemporary was lacking. He failed to see that all along the pattern of creation and creator, which has at its disposal the greatest energies of transformation and renewal of which the human being is capable, had potentially changed the whole of his relationship with creation and the creator and, one believes, even that of creation and the creator of the human being. The vision of a kind of partnership which came to him encoded perhaps first in a dream, the dream of Jacob's ladder – a dream also dreamt in a great wasteland of the spirit – was at last fulfilled and waiting, and the same reinvestment of power that was uniquely at the disposal of what Odysseus would have called the gods ready to be transferred to man, and man's whole estate in creation could be altered by being entrusted in a measure with a greater role and responsibility in making life on earth mortally immortal, and divine. What had been regarded as of the gods on Olympus and in the heavens was within the deepest longing of the human soul at last ready for an immortal mortality.

Jung, in his great hypothesis of the collective unconscious, which explains so much of what had been inexplicable in the phenomenon of the spirit and the thrust of human history, gives it its contemporary name of 'individuation', and already, for some three thousand years, the Odyssean journey has been there as the intuitive anticipation of what the process of differentiation which man had to achieve in his quest for individuation is to the psychologist-in-depth today. Now, with the physical world known and exposed to the vision of man, magnified with all the scientific and technological resources for enlarging external perceptions, laid out in the sun like some mysterious animal hunted in the forests of the night, skinned and ready for carving up as nourishment for the greedy materialistic spirit of the day, and even Shakespeare's visiting moon walked on as a doorstep to another thrust of exploration into the expanding universe, it is being matched by an even more meaningful act of discovery in the objective universe within and its collective unconscious, spread out like another night sky in human imagination. It is perhaps the most meaningful journey of discovery ever undertaken by man, because this thrust into the universe without depends ultimately on being contained by the thrust into the world within. This law, as it were, of infinite compensation has to be obeyed if the human spirit is not again to be thrown out of balance and to go on producing these hubrises of the most lethal and destructive kind that already imperil the world scene. There may be no specific myth, no specific prophecy to outline for the exploring spirit the way that lies ahead, as Teiresias did for Odysseus. But in a sense all the myths that have ever been are sufficient to bring man to where, at the end of the journey, he is fulfilled in the keeping of his own 'prophetic soul . . . dreaming on things to come', out of which the blind seer came to set him on course. We all have such a dimension and such a seer.

There, as in all moments of darkness and arrested development and, in the world of appearances and of floating things, as the Zen Buddhists call it, nothing but the chaos and old night that was in the beginning facing our deprived, rational selves, there is in this dreaming other self the direction that is necessary to recognize the call to individuation and its fulfilment in a truly modern way. This potential of modern man on a quest of soul and a resumption of the dynamic dialogue between himself and the greater self is there always, like a star in the mirror of another self within, if only he would look not just with a blink of one-eyed science, as Blake named it, but with both inner and outer eyes.

The detail of this statement and its validity need no amplification here, because they have already been confirmed in the natural science of analytical psychology and increasingly in the thrust of physics, and are, or should be, part of the intellectual and spiritual equipment of every modern man, because without these he is modern only in a technical sense and still archaic and unsynchronized in the demands of his lifetime. So the name of individuation itself should be enough guidance. It is written large in letters of flame within the awakening imagination, as a signpost at a vital crossroads in the story of man, and could hardly be missed.

For Jung this immense potential of individuation in the human being was already expressed naturally and intuitively in the example of Christ. He would say to me that in a very real sense there had only been one modern man, and he was crucified two thousand years ago. And he would emphasize that the great fallacy, in so far as the example of Christ was an anticipation of what he meant by individuation and differentiation, was that it had been taken literally and not in its full symbolic and synchronistic meaning, and men and the churches had advocated blind imitation of

71

Christ, whereas the real meaning of His message to man was that he had to live his own natural individual nature and the gifts with which he had been endowed as truthfully as Christ had lived the end to which He had been born.

Jung was himself an enormous source of reassurance, for his whole life was a tremendous act of confirmation of what is needed and will come. Towards the end of his life he would tell me how people would often write to him and importune him to define and elaborate on what God was and what God meant to him, and in the end he felt the only way he could answer the question was to say: 'I cannot define God as an idea or a concept because I am just an old African these days, who finds God in his dreams.'

I could not say all this with the certainty I feel were it not for the blessing of providence which linked me from childhood with the imagination of a first people of life, and by following this imagination, and all the 'Once upon a time...' things it brought alive in my spirit, the chain between the beginning of life on earth and my own 'now' and what has to come has not been broken. It is for this reason I believe that my experience of the little memory and the great memory could have some objective value in an age so without beginning and climatic awareness of continuity. Even in moments when I have been under what appeared to be an irrevocable sentence of death, I never lost even the frailest link in the chain between the beginning and me, and hence the now.

I remember in particular a night in a cell in a prison at a place called in Malay 'The Earth of Desire' when a Japanese guard, who had been very good to me at great risk to himself, told me that he feared I was to be executed early the next morning, and when I asked him if that was 'For sure?' he said I must know by now that he had never deceived me as others had done. 'This time,' he went on, using a phrase one hears so often in Japan, with an intonation like the whisper of an autumn leaf breaking free from its outpost at the top of a high tree and surrendering itself to the first command of winter, releasing its hold to make for the sodden earth below, 'it cannot be helped.'

I stood at the small window in the cell-like room in which I was confined as the evening storm of thunder and rain broke outside. The storm appeared with such regularity every evening that I could have set a watch by it. The wonder of it was that it gave one the most convincing demonstration of the orderly succession of harmony within the nature of all things, because always there was first the lightning, purple and with an almost audible swish as if the inflammable silk of darkness had been set alight. Then came the thunder, and after the thunder the rain, and with it all the smell of the earth, and all rooted within it taking new heart for another day of life refreshed and renewed.

For me it was like that thunder in the beginning when the Hottentot voice called out and told his Griqua companions to listen because the voice of the thunder was the voice of their God. And an immense sense of resolution went through me, an awareness that even the Japanese at the moment of their greatest power were subjects, and not in command of the creation that came in this measure and order of the lightning, the thunder and the rain. And I went and slept well on the wooden board that night.

So all that I have written in this short account of what a 'Once upon a time . . .' race contributed to continuity and illumination of my own Odyssean pattern seemed to compel recording also what follows, in the hope that perhaps others with their own patterns apparently so dangerously arrested too would turn to this other journey which is there, in the keeping prophetic in every authentic Odyssean journey of the soul. We would all be doing only what man at the beginning was charged to do in his own great unknown and perilous context of the greatest and darkest continent, Africa, reminding himself as he reminded me always: 'There is a dream dreaming us.'

And as he spoke there in this immense waterless wasteland that was his home, which for millennia had been far kinder to him than our cushioned and padded civilization, still destroying him and his kind, I realized that the Bushman was rich in a way that I was poor. He had at that moment nothing on him that was not necessary to secure his survival from birth to death. He was so deprived of what we in the world would have regarded as essentials, and yet his whole presence and the expression on his face and in those antique eyes was so full of life and light that I wanted to lay my hand upon my heart and confess with a certain anguish that the difference between us could simply be that I *had*, and he *was*, to such an extent that in the sense of a dream dreaming us there was nowhere in the vast wastelands, forests and mountains of Africa where he felt alone, unaccompanied or unobserved. Indeed, this 'is-ness' of his was so great that there was nowhere he went, I had learnt, where he did not feel known, so much so that when a star fell in one of those great arcs of descent which is only possible in the heavens of the southern hemisphere that are the incomparable seal and ceiling of the temple of the night, he knew it was on a journey to report to those whom he referred to as 'walking on their feet upright and feeling themselves upright', that one other who too had been 'walking upright and feeling upright had fallen over on to his side', and that 'a wind would come to remove his footsteps from the sand so they would not confuse those who were still walking on their feet upright and make them think that he was still upright'.

When there was a period of great rainlessness and a

scorching of the earth by the sun, the prompting of this prophetic dimension within would send him apart at a critical moment of a hunt for food to sit in the dark shadow of a great acacia tree, and his companions would make us all halt and tell us not to disturb him because there in the cool he was doing work of great importance: making clouds for the rain to come.

Then there came a night of one of the most beautiful full moons, ranking first perhaps in the great moon collection in my own imagination, when a small group, still integrated in the heart of the desert in their stone-age culture, danced with a passion and perseverance that in the end began to strain even my love of their rituals. And I asked why and how much longer they were going to go on dancing like that. And the answer came: 'You see that the moon is full and feels itself to be utterly full? But it is about to wane and will be in danger of waning utterly and not coming back unless we show it how full our hearts are of the moon and utterly long for it to return.'

There were other examples to illustrate why I felt they were rich, why they seemed to have a life full of meaning and importance, because how could they not, believing they had within them the power of making clouds and influencing the movement of the moon and the tides it drew not only within their hearts and in seas they had never seen but also in the sap of all the trees and plants which surrounded them, as well as in the blood of the world of animals sending some of them still to bay like dogs the moment it appeared above the rim of the desert. All this came together in a flash, and it was part of the vividness and clearcut identity which I saw in him and heightened the quality of belonging I have described. He never seemed to be deprived of meaning or to suffer the feeling of helplessness and insecurity which increasingly haunts civilized man, although secure as he has never been before of physical life and its survival. These feelings are all part and proof of the evocation and intimation which come to one naturally out of this climate of the spirit which accompanies one at birth and presides also over the last season of life and, I am certain, as Odysseus must have been certain after his sacrifice to all the gods, presides also over the beyond.

And this last reference to what presides over the beyond and Odysseus's final certainty brings me to a meaning of the Homeric imagery which I have not touched on before, because it lends itself even less than the specific symbolism with which I have been concerned to any lucid summarization of the interpretations and the dimension into which it leads my own spirit and imagination.

It is all rooted in the fact that by tradition both Homer and Teiresias were blind. It has always seemed to me that in choosing Teiresias to speak for his own prophetic soul, influenced as Homer must have been by the incomparable standing of the man as seer and prophet, the decisive element which forced his imagination to select Teiresias for this profound personification was his blindness. By the complex and stubborn tradition which comes out of an era of Greek history where the mythological and the historical are incapable of meaningful separation, we know that neither of them was born blind. Something immensely traumatic happened to them in life which made them blind, and compelled them not only to turn away from the everyday trivialities and eventfulness of the life of their time, but to perceive where the destiny of life on earth and origin even before the great mythological beginning are one in the blueprint of pre-meaning. It is as if, by being blind to the present, they both would see more clearly what had been and was to come.

As far as Teiresias is concerned, I myself who am no

scholar could write a small essay about the symbolism and imagery of his life in the context of the disintegration of the great Theban empire, which was one of the greatest the world has ever seen, and its shattering consequences, many of which have such disturbing parallels with our own day, as for instance the impact of the coming of Bacchus and the proliferation of drugs on a worldwide scale in the life of our own time. So much so that on re-reading Euripides' *Bacchae* the other day and finding that the first emissary of the coming and spread of the spirit of Bacchus is 'a city slicker with a smooth tongue', the distance between Thebes and my own metropolitan world ceased to exist.

I could in particular in this epic of *The Iliad* and *The Odyssey*, which in essence is so much about the role of the feminine, of the woman in the life of man, and the right as yet denied to her to be also her own feminine self beyond the purely biological role of begetting, stress how one tradition holds that Teiresias was struck blind because he saw Pallas Athena bathing in the nude, and was thought as having spied upon her. It would seem thus as if a prophet too had to be aware of the profound ambivalence of his calling, which made him not only without honour in his own country but also without honour in the world of the gods he had to serve, if he assumed too much for his vision and ignored its relationship to time and the fact that the readiness of life and creation to receive it was not always there.

Yet what was outwardly and physically a tragedy, was inwardly a source of great strength, because nothing could have made the prophet more aware of the immeasurable significance of the role of this goddess, who was by far the most differentiated of all goddesses in the Greek heaven, and in particular in *The Odyssey*, since from the beginning to the end, Pallas Athena had taken Odysseus himself singularly into her keeping. If it had not been for her constant love and care, her advocacy with her father Zeus in heaven, her solicitude and ingenuity and planning and intervening on his behalf, he would never have returned safely to Ithaca and, what is more, even if he had returned, could have lost the final battle in the great hall and the streets without. If anybody doubts how much *The Odyssey* is a search of man for his neglected and as yet unlived feminine self, this presence throughout of Pallas Athena should remove it. How advanced an image of the feminine she was already is shown by the fact that in the beginning she was allotted a twin sister, whom she loved dearly, since her many-sidedness of being could not be fully expressed in one.

Tradition sheds no light on how Homer, whose life across the ages has been associated with so many of the great cities of Greece, and which was obviously an immensely diverse and eventful one, was blinded. No tradition that I know of helps one's guess as to why he too was made blind. For myself, I have always had a hunch that the symbolic nature of the life of a great artist and seer demanded so constant and concentrated a vision of the invisible realities of life and meaning that the vision of life in the external world had to be sacrificed, so that all those visual energies and capacities could be withdrawn from it and devoted solely to bringing utter totality and precision to the inner vision.

And then, of course, the blindness would have had great compensation in the immunity it conferred against the temptations of the world and its glitter, and still so strangely unready and even antagonistic towards all that Homer, like Teiresias, saw so clearly. Serving as they did the great imponderable of an invisible reality, they were in a dimension where only the blind could lead the blind and show one another how to prepare the spirit and imagination of man, like a ploughed field, for the seeds of change and increase which would come to them in the shape of a story and the great song of *The Iliad* and *The Odyssey*.

In reading and re-reading *The Odyssey* in so many different translations (because, alas, I had no Greek at all) I have come to feel more and more how important was the symbolism of the shared blindness in the poem. Increasingly it seemed to me that the artist had a special subjective bond with this other prophetic figure in his story, a bond which came near to surpassing the distance which had to be maintained between the creator and the created in order to make what was created fully valid in its own right and destiny. There seemed to me thus an emphasis on Teiresias unique among the many characters in *The Odyssey*, as if this were not only a product of the commitment demanded of one of the greatest poets of all time by his art, but also a commitment and testimony and special advocacy by the artist as a man who had experienced the life of his time profoundly and been stricken blind in its service. So from the first meeting with Odysseus in Hades, in the world of the undiscovered dimensions of the collective unconscious, Teiresias was there not only as ambassador of life but spokesman of Homer the man, overwhelmed by private and personal duty of artist, seer and creator to be obedient to their greatest awareness, not only of the art and the prophecy but also the future of the human species and its unfulfilled task of becoming truly and totally human.

All my own certainty about the great certitudes of Odysseus and life in Ithaca after his return from the main is based, I know, on a personal and private interpretation, which I had to obey because it came to me purely from the story itself and from knowing how dependent the increase of a sense of meaning in life is on obedience to the new awarenesses that come of their own accord in this way. There are moments even when the memories of my many readings congregate, and I have visions of Odysseus in the last year of his life on Ithaca, sitting perhaps exactly where his faithful old swineherd sat in the long years when he himself had vanished from his island into the Trojan conflict and, although the island was full of rumours of the burning of the topless towers of Ilium and stories of the return of other heroes who had survived the battles on the great plain, yet nobody knew what had happened to Odysseus. But something in this humblest of Odysseus's servants, somewhere still blindly believing, made him watch and wait for a sign that his master would still, despite all appearances, be about to come home again. There Odysseus too would scan the same horizon for what was beyond the moment when his end would come to him gently, like a mist out of that same wine-red sea, as the vision of Aphrodite had once unwound itself from its smoking waters in a rose-stained dawn.

All this and more seems to me to add to the weight as real evidence of the Teiresian journey of Odysseus. Certainly there is also this objective evidence to support my interpretation of the significance of this strangely-twinned blindness in the Homeric story, and how it was an essential ingredient for heightening the perception of prophet and poet of unfulfilled reality pitched in the future.

And here, as I am rounding my own story in a return to my own beginnings, an example of what I mean came to me, as so often in my reading of Greek mythology, out of the heart of my native continent. It happened one night in the northeast part of central Africa, somewhere between Fort Johnson and Broken Hill, almost fifty years ago – a time when one still had to travel with porters through that part of Africa, as Livingstone and Stanley had done. One of the most rewarding parts of the journey was the moment spent with all the bearers, some seventy of them, round the central fire of our camp, and the conversation which passed between us all, conversation, I need hardly repeat, of people who had no other art but the art of the living word on the living tongue.

There one night they were talking about an African people on whose frontiers we were travelling, and listening to stories of how cultured they were in the African definition of the term. They spoke of how in particular they were dedicated to music and most especially to singing, to such an extent that chiefs and sub-chiefs rivalled one another in having singers of distinction as part of their clans and groups, and would conspire and cheat one another to attract artists of note to their beehive courts in the bush.

They mentioned one paramount chief who valued his singers to such an extent that the most distinguished singer of all had his eyes put out in the belief that, being blind, he would not allow himself to be enticed to strange parts of the country and people he did not know, but would stay on at the paramount chief's court to the end of his days.

I, in some horror at so extreme a deed, said: 'But what good would that have been, because surely a person subjected to such horror would stop singing forever?'

'Ah, no!' There was a chorus of replies, almost dismissing me with notes of unbelief that I should be so naive about the nature of life. Several voices rushed in to explain: 'Surely you should know what such men are. Born to sing, when the pain of being blind has gone and in experiencing all the affection and attention paid to them more than ever, one day they will suddenly start singing again, and everybody would listen with their hearts beating faster and their eyes wet with tears, because they would never have heard such beauty of singing before.'

Even more convincing to me, and a very precious part of what birds have done for me and my own Odyssean awareness in life, is something that happened some five years later in Hokkaido, the north part of Japan which still contains remnants of its aboriginal population. I landed with a remarkable Japanese friend at a little port on the north island one morning on a brilliant early spring day. The sea was calm; no day could have looked more peaceful and ready for the spring and implicit with singularity as if marked out specially by fate.

Although we did not know it yet, at that very moment an immense tidal wave, which had been started by an undersea eruption off the coast of Peru days before, was bearing down on that part of the coast and, half an hour after we had left the port, overwhelmed it and drowned many of its inhabitants. Very soon afterwards the sky darkened and became stormy, and towards evening a full-scale blizzard set in. By the time we got to the capital, Sapporo, and the shelter of its biggest hotel, we were soaked and miserable. We went to our rooms, changed quickly, and came down into the large lounge crowded with people, and sat down to order some very hot refreshment.

We had hardly sat down when a crowd of people appeared with musical instruments of all kinds at the reception desk, and the whisper went round that it was the Boston Symphony Orchestra arriving, and that they would be giving a concert later that night. The conversation at that moment was loud, lively and uncontrolled to the point of being almost offensive, yet it could not have been more appropriate for the impact of synchronicity which followed. For suddenly, from the corner of the room behind me, a bird began to sing, and it sang with such beauty and such clarity and such authority that the whole room went silent. I have never heard a bird song more beautiful. Both my friend and I were almost at once in tears. The immense power of the music had an almost paranormal quality of command that was supreme, because it was not an expression of power itself but came purely from what the music was within itself; an expression rather of ultimate harmony and beauty, asserting itself in its most vulnerable and defenceless form, relying for its own authority and impact solely on the beauty and its necessities of order and measure and the lucidity of its voice.

I do not know for how long the bird sang, but the silence was unbroken. Not a teaspoon made a glass or cup tinkle, not a whisper, not a clatter of crockery or trays being laid out in the great kitchen came there to disturb it. We might have been in the same great wood where the nightingales once sang to Keats, or indeed to Eliot, and made him think of how their silver siftings could have fallen to stain Agamemnon's stiff dishonoured shroud. It was a moment utterly timeless in a way that could not be misunderstood, because it was free of all physical and material barriers and impediments of personal pain and injury, as if it were fulfilling directly the measure of the will of creation invested in that little body of a small bird, un-wounding itself there and regaining its full sense of being, with its heart in its throat. The memory stays as the most precious of the many recollections of bird memories that I have treasured, more precious even than the memory of the honey-guide which was so constant a messenger of the materialization of Eros in the dark heart of the African bush.

I thought of Lear's great statement to Cordelia, about how free they would be in prison and sing like birds in a cage, and remarked to my companion that I felt the bird could never have sung so beautifully if it had not spent so much of its life in a cage. He agreed, but then spoke in that soft, what I called *mono-no-aware* tone of voice of his, the *mono-no-aware* quality being the element in the Japanese spirit which makes them aware of how deep down in the nature of all things there is a clear bond of infinite sympathy which neither diversity of species nor character nor even sheer being can prevent:

'Yes, it is true that keeping that little bird in the cage always helps the song. But what helps it more than anything else is the fact that the little bird has been blinded early on as well, and somehow needed this double separation from the world to add to the beauty of its singing.'

After experiences such as these, I felt more than ever that only the image of the blind Teiresias could have thrown light on this dark area of Homer himself and spoken for him, as he himself could not have done, and so created this certainty he alone could not give for the end of that other journey within *The Odyssey*.

And so, drought-stricken and deprived of myths and healing imagery as our time in this bleak climate of the spirit may appear to be, one does not doubt that for those who have kept faith with their own odyssey all the gods in Olympus, even in their diminished Roman role among the stars of outer space, and their total absence in the conscious patter which passes for a dialogue with the self in the rhinestone glitter of the contemporary scene, will not have vanished. They are where they have always been, serving the cause of creation, night and day, with the dreams and visions needed for accomplishing the sanity and wholeness demanded by the task of individuation, and so increasing the range and quality of the partnership between the individual and creation.

Here there are no words to carry on the theme: it has to be lived before it can be known and the relevant words come to express it. Only the abiding imagery to lead us on remains unblurred, and among these the final image is also the first image. It lives for me in that timeless moment when there was a flash of the long lightning of the vast interior of Africa and I heard the first voice of the thunder that followed and, hard on that, one of those dear Griqua-Hottentot voices, also a fragment of one of the most ancient races in Africa, commanding his fellows to listen, because it was the voice of their God. And it is because, ever since, I believe, I have tried to listen, as attentively as it was in my power and capacity to listen, that I have ventured on rendering this account of what such listening has done to me, leaving me with a hope that could only vanish if ever the thunder lost its voice and ceased to speak.

The Little Memory

'O man, remember!'
Upanishads

I SEEM TO HAVE been born into a special relationship with the Kalahari. This relationship came into its most acute and essential human focus through the Bushman and what I came to know of the last fragments of his great stone-age civilization which had survived relatively intact in the heart of the desert, as I have described it in *The Lost World of the Kalahari*. But it was preceded by an intense attraction which the Kalahari had for me from the moment I first heard the members of my large family exchanging information and experiences of it with one another. My grandfather, whose memory was so prodigious that he could give me a detailed, first-hand description of a battle in which he fought against the British in 1848, had vivid accounts of several probes into the desert round about the middle of the last century. Our history books were full of the adventures of missionaries, Hottentots, hunters and colourful pioneering individualists who had penetrated more deeply into its unknown interior than even the 'Sutho peoples who had established themselves along its more fertile and dependable fringes. The fact that most of it was still a vast unknown, despite some established routes across it, was enough to excite my imagination as a child, as indeed it had excited the imagination of one of my favourite authors in my father's library, the great Jules Verne. His own abundant, highly intuitive and, in a scientific sense, prophetic fantasy had already inspired stories of British and German navies battling or 'grappling with one another', as the caption for the illustrations had it, on what was inked in bright blue on our maps as one of the great lakes of Africa, the Lake Ngami I was to know so well myself. Jules Verne had done his homework thoroughly, and on one of the expeditions prominently featured in his fiction were some quarrelsome European intruders already accompanied by a Bushman guide.

Then our general sense of mystery about the Kalahari was heightened later, towards the end of the nineteenth century, by a spurious American showman, Farini, who went on an expedition along the southwestern and western fringes of the Kalahari and claimed at length and with great plausibility to have discovered the ruins of a lost city in the desert. Lots of people took him at his word. In my youth the newspapers from time to time carried special pieces about yet another expedition which had followed in Farini's footsteps and come back without having discovered any traces of the lost city, yet, paradoxically, convinced more than ever of its existence. It is only now that Farini has been thoroughly discredited, as he should have been ages ago had he not received the benefit of the doubt for so long because of the capacity of a vast, unexplored wasteland to prevent any speculation about its secrets, however extreme, from being finally disproved.

The climate of fantasy and wonder created about the Kalahari in this and many other ways was more than enough to excite the imagination of any child, but fired mine more than most because it had two substantial interests denied most others to ignite it. One, of course, was my profound preoccupation with the Bushman; the other, the fact that my family had come to own a vast amount of land in the southernmost area of the desert where it overflowed the borders of Bechuanaland, as it was called in those days, beyond the Molopo and Nosop rivers.

This had come about because the discovery of diamonds at Kimberley and in other parts of southern Africa, as well as gold on the Witwatersrand, had implanted in the minds not only of South Africa but of the wider world a vision of the earth of southern Africa as the roof over an immense Aladdin's cave of precious stones and rainbow minerals. For decades shiploads of people, compelled to follow this vision, came pouring into southern Africa, and even the people of southern Africa, whose history might have given them some immunity against so lustful a dream, shared this vision to such an extent that those who could afford it bought up unclaimed land on the extremities of the inhabited colonies in the belief that it too would be found one day to conceal hoards of treasure.

My own father, who as a lawyer had been involved with many of the more successful individuals and odd companies associated with the stampede for instant wealth, founded a syndicate to buy a huge spread of land between the settled frontiers of the Cape Colony and what became the Bechuanaland Protectorate. From a farming point of view this land, which was really an unappetizing overflow of the Kalahari Desert, was rated so low that, if I remember rightly, my father paid no more than a penny an acre for his share. It says a great deal for the power of this vision of diamonds and gold from the earth that my father bought the land without seeing it, and knowing little more than what was included in the reports of the geologists who had surveyed those far northern districts of the Cape.

Elsewhere in southern Africa some local tradition, indigenous legend or extraordinary physical feature would help geologists and surveyors to dignify plots of land not just with numbers but with names. In this northwestern world of the Cape and the southwestern fringes of the real Kalahari Desert, however, there seemed to be neither people

91

nor history nor special feature to provide suitable names. Consequently surveyors drew on their own fancy for baptizing these slices of geometrically carved-up earth. The geologist who was responsible for the area where my father purchased his land, for instance, began by calling the plots after cheeses he had eaten and come to relish. Thus my father's main purchase gloried in the name of Stilton, which had delighted my French grandmother, whom I never knew, because 'le Stilton', she had once declared, was perhaps the only good thing the English had ever contributed to civilization. When the cheeses the geologist could recall ran out, he drew on titles of books by his favourite writers, notably Sir Walter Scott, and the land belonging to our syndicate therefore included lots like 'Ivanhoe', 'Durward', 'Waverley', 'Kenilworth' and so on, until Scott gave out too and Kingsley appeared on the scene with 'Westward Ho!'.

But once the purchase of this land had been completed, and the names and title deeds registered, my father appears to have shown no further interest in it for some twenty years or more, and it was not until 1913, some nine months before his death, that he decided he would go and have a look at this land which had haunted our imagination for so long. An elder brother and I accompanied him, and the jealousy and envy set up by my inclusion at the age of seven in so privileged a project was assuaged by the parental declaration that it was an exhausting journey along a road which led through a long succession of gates, and I was physically adroitly sprung, tough, and an ardent and tireless opener of gates.

So in the spring of 1913 we set off in a four-wheeled vehicle known as a Spider, which was usually reserved for my mother and visiting ladies because it was more comfortable than the two-wheeled Cape carts used in our part of the interior when the normal mode, for men, of travelling on horseback was not possible. At the time I thought no more of it than that it was chosen for my father's comfort, but know now that this squeamish form of travel was a sign of how his health was already beginning to fail and would lead to his death not long after. The journey made such a deep impression on me that its outline is unforgettable, although many of the names of the people on the way and petty details have been overlaid. As usual, we were not bothered by the fact that, with the exception of two little marketing places on the way, there would be no hotels or inns in which to stay. We knew that we could commit ourselves to the deep-rooted tradition of hospitality and a kind of obligatory respect among the Afrikaner people of the interior for the stranger who called on them for food and shelter. We were joyfully received for break-fast, coffee breaks, afternoon teas and finally dinner, bed and again breakfast, at farms from the most luxurious to the humblest – if anything most joyfully and, for me, enter-tainingly at the humblest. Whenever we felt in need of refreshment we would just follow the first track branching out from our own road, pathways we called 'little coffee tracks' because we knew that where the track found the inevitable homestead there would at the very least be some coffee, hot in a large enamel pot on the kitchen range, and masses of rusks, or even our national version of the brioche our Huguenot forefathers had brought with them from Navarre, in the larder waiting to be warmed up for us.

Endearing as this all was, so that to this day the memory of it is like an aisle of candlelight in the dark behind me, the overwhelming experience for me began when we left the world of homesteads behind us, slept at night under the stars beside the Spider, and wherever we looked by day saw nothing but the sandveld around us, with the bush giving way to grass – fresh after the first spasmodic rain of spring

– going silk, satin or velvet according to the strength behind the swipes which the paw of the wind took at it, and over all the cloudless blue, and here and there some hawk or vulture rising on quivering wings to the foretop of the day from where no movement of life from horizon to horizon on the earth below could escape its eyes. Often sections of the earth itself were transformed as if into coats of arms, because a quartered view would be made heraldic by the silhouette of the purple and black gemsbok and his long double spear of horn, supported by our only gazelle, a lone springbuck rampant, while in the far background where the blue of the morning combined with the blue of sky and the blue of distance to form a greater blue, substantial as a drift of woodsmoke on an early stir of air, the shapes of the herd from which he was separate and singular lost their outlines and only their colours were flicker and flame of the fire of their being, adding to the overwhelming act of translation in which the day of full sun was already engaged.

As a result, this emancipation of earth and grass and birds from the world of men was immediate intoxication, which put me firmly on the road to becoming an incurable desert addict. When, on our second and third days, the world of grass and open veld gradually merged into what appeared a vast parkland of camelthorn trees, which from then on became for me the greatest of all the many kinds of acacia that ever fought the recurring droughts of Africa in order to grace the heat of its days with shade, an odd, homeward-bound feeling began to invade me and, I believe, even to quicken the pace of our tired horses until, when at last we found the relevant 'Stilton' surveyors' beacons, it had become a complete and established fact in my emotions. Those beacons moved me particularly because they resembled the little Hottentot cairns of stone at home, raised there, as everywhere else in southern Africa, in praise and remembrance of their god, Heitse-Eibib, whose voice they believed was in the sound which the wind of morning made in the leaves of our thorn trees and swinging grass. No well-found estate surrounded by parks in Britain could have made me richer or prouder in belonging to a family who had such earth in their keeping.

Young as I was, and although knowing that I had never been in that world before, I was increasingly convinced from thereon that it was my kind of world. It was my first encounter with a dimension of memory which has haunted me all my life – a phenomenon which one knows perhaps best as a child, loses in the process of being educated into the here and now which is our brief, provisional home, and only tends to recover as one enters the last of our allotment of seasons. It is an overarching memory which does not belong to man so much as to life itself, and no matter how much one may forget and ignore it, it never forgets or ignores whatever form of being is invested with life. It is a memory of all the life that has ever been; it is imparted to one through natural instinct and feeling, and yet it is also full of premonition of the future, and more. For my part, I can only say that to the extent to which I had become aware of it through the play of instinct and feeling in myself and intimations of dreams and images coming to me unsolicited and of their own accord – strong, real and often contradictory to all that the world and time surrounding me demanded – it remained somewhere and somehow in supreme command of all that I possessed of meaning. I came to call it to myself the Great Memory.

When one took the span of the four score and ten years which the psalmist prescribes as our maximum allotment and compared it with this vast input of true and proven experience recorded in this long history of life even before the Word, it shrank to the littlest of a little. I was, of course, totally incapable of putting any of this in words at the time, but am certain I am expressing some of the impact of my first experience of the desert, and the sense of innermost awakening, clear and imperative as a call of reveille on a trumpet at first light summoning its cavalry out of a dream of sleep.

And then there was something else that went with it and came alive when we talked about it at night by our fire and I listened to the old pioneer who had joined us as guide and knew the Kalahari intimately. He spoke simply and eloquently of how it was a desert only in the sense that it had no water on the surface, and above all he told us of the courage of the earth, its plants and animals, and how they fought the sun and searing winds of summer, the dust and frost of winter, the long months and, at times, years without rain, to maintain themselves in the abundance and beauty which clothed all the forms of vivid life that we saw around us. Wonderful as the earth of Africa was in all its profuse and diverse statements, this desert earth, described around that fire, became miraculous. This experience was the seed of an awareness of the abiding miracle of the despised and the rejected in nature becoming a unique temple of life to come, a living testimony to a promise implicit in creation that life, no matter how tested and challenged by anti-life, would always be triumphant, and that where and when the challenge of anti-life, the tensions and conflict, were greatest, the sweetest of flowers and fruit and the most rare and precious statements of beauty of sky and earth would justify and resolve them. I came to call it Cinderella earth, and, in the long years that followed, this image was never displaced but only grew more evocative and relevant.

So the greater memory would have it beyond doubt that this relationship with the Kalahari I have described began in a measureless primordial past, while the lesser memory would give it a time and what soldiers call a map reference of the place of the birth of consciousness of this relationship, and base it firmly around our final fire on that journey with my father in his last spring of 1913. In this there was for once no contradiction or paradox between the two memories. Both combined and were at one to give me from that moment on the sense of belonging in general to the Cinderella earth of the world, and most specifically to the formidable land which had unbent to make us welcome in a vast park of giraffe acacias and their wide and thick carpets of shade.

In the years that followed there were other occasions when I came to see more of the Kalahari along its perimeters, and all that I saw increased its attraction for me. The people who had come to occupy its more hospitable parts belonged to the great 'Sutho complex of Bantu nations who had been forced to give way before the Zulu and Matabele imperialisms which ravaged the central areas of southern Africa at the end of the eighteenth and beginning of the nineteenth centuries, and established themselves in remoter areas of the continent, less fertile and less well watered but easier to defend. At home most of the people who worked on my mother's and my grandfather's farms were 'Sutho families from Basutoland – now Lesotho – who had come with their own cattle and sheep on a three-yearly rotation to help us run our own great spread of sheep- and cattle-land. I had come to know them better than any of the other black races of our continent and naturally took to their kinsmen who inhabited the most northern, eastern and southwestern Kalahari marches. They tended to be organized in tribes, well rooted in their history, social evolution and traditions, and produced some of the most remarkable chiefs in African history: men like Kham the Great,

Sibele and Linchwe, whose stories, as related to me by our own 'Sutho workers, caused me in my spare time, holidays and early working life to seek them out and get to know them better.

In particular I made friends with a remarkable Botswana tribe called the Bakhatla – Men of the Baboon. My first visit to the Bakhatla coincided with the death of their paramount chief. His heir and successor, Molefi, was still only a child and, as tradition demanded, the dead chief's brother, Isang, was called to act as regent until Molefi grew old enough to take over the chieftainship. I found myself drawn to Isang. He was highly intelligent, wise, energetic and, for a man stretched between the pagan traditions of 'Sutho culture, still profound and powerful around him, and the dour, official Christian religion to which they had been converted, he retained a cohesion of personality and an integrity I thought as remarkable as it was honourable.

One of the first things Isang did after assuming the regency was to tackle the real, material problems of his tribe, the greatest of which were created by the lack of permanent water and erratic cycles of rain. He had called in water diviners and geologists to survey the land for artesian water and started drilling operations on a progressive scale. Unfortunately this policy brought him quickly into conflict with the Bakhatla's most powerful witchdoctors. The witchdoctors maintained that, if life had meant the Bakhatla to have more sources of permanent water, God and the spirits would have provided them in the shape of natural springs and rivers, and that to try and force the earth to yield up its secret water was active blasphemy and would antagonize the spirits to such an extent that they would interfere with the fall of rain on Bakhatla earth. To what extent the witchdoctors were sincere in making this their reason for opposing Isang's drilling policy, or whether they were just using it as a pretext for getting rid of him, will never be known. It was probably a mixture of both. Nonetheless, their hatred of Isang alone had become great enough for them to have opposed him by any other means had this course failed them, and was due to the fact that he not only ignored them but seemed to think them a retrograde influence on the people and an impediment to progress. He himself declared openly that, as a Christian, he did not believe in witchcraft and other superstitious practices. As a Christian in a tribe where polygamy was practised by all who could afford it, for instance, he had only one wife and was scrupulously monogamous.

Unfortunately for Isang, when the quarrel between him and the witchdoctors was at its most intense, the rains began to fail. It was no use Isang pointing out that this was a recurring pattern in the history of Kalahari earth. The witchdoctors declared it was because he had angered the spirits, as they had foretold. Moreover, they added, the spirits were so outraged that they would see to it that no rain fell until Isang was deposed. And for some years the rains failed utterly. The effect of this on a people for whom rain mattered so much was decisive. Their greeting to one another was the 'Sutho word for rain, 'pula'. Their farewell to one another was the same, 'pula', uttered with the implicit wish that wherever one went it would rain upon one. To hear the cry 'Pula!' go up at their tribal assemblies was like a hallelujah at the beginning of a great oratorio. So none of us who knew the Bakhatla was surprised that the anti-Isang mood, despite all the manifest good he had done for his people, became so intense that the witchdoctors issued a warning to the Bakhatla: if they wanted the drought to end, they would have to bring forward young Molefi's inauguration as paramount chief and depose Isang. Popular support for the idea soon persuaded Isang that he would have to give way if the Bakhatla were not to be torn apart in a quarrel that could even lead to civil war. So although Molefi was only just over sixteen and still, by tradition, had some years to wait, it was decided that he would be installed, not on a day appointed by the regent, as would have been normal, but by the witchdoctors, who claimed that on the very day it happened the rain would fall.

This audacious prophecy was made many months before the day fixed for the inauguration, and it was considered so dramatic and awesome that news of it was spread by rumour among all the 'Sutho tribes of Botswana and their kinsmen working abroad. It even reached me in the Cape, where I was working at the time. The Old Testament nature of the subject of the rumour, the conflict of the instinctive and natural with the cultured and the contrived, between the primordial and the immediate, stirred my imagination at its deepest level and combined with this commitment to the Kalahari world with which I had started, and the great memory with which it was associated, to make me resolve to witness Isang's abdication and Molefi's inauguration.

I had so much urgent work to do at the time that I had to cancel my first thoughts of spending a week or two among the Bakhatla beforehand. Hard as I tried, I could not get to Mochudi, their capital, until the late afternoon of the day before the inauguration. As my train drew nearer to Palapye Road, a dusty and windswept little siding that was my destination after a journey from the Cape of two days and two nights, the evidence of how grim a drought had been inflicted on the Bakhatla multiplied rapidly. The scene, never one with much fat upon it, was so lean that instinctively an image of our mother earth as a dying person came to me and I was looking at it as in T. S. Eliot's description of obsession with death:

100

The skull beneath the skin,
And breastless creatures under ground,
Leaned backward with a lipless grin.

Even the thorn trees, which somehow in my recollection of the past had always managed to hold some gallant little blade of green jealously guarded between their long spikes of pointed white thorn, and were for me the earth's living badge of courage, had gone black with lack of moisture. Everywhere I looked the fitful afternoon wind was lifting a haze, or at times raising a smoke, of fine dust to deprive the day utterly of its blue and stain all that was upon the earth the same colour of burnt-out ash. Often the whiff of carcasses of the dead and rotting animals would come through my carriage windows on their intake of hot air, in the sullen light of a sulphur sun. However misguided the supernatural explanations of the drought might still have been to sceptical European sensibilities, the evidence of its effect and the increasing devastation of the scene made me fear as I had not feared since my experience of the great drought of 1911. It is fear no European can know or understand, because it is a compound of horror, dread and hopelessness which is more of the blood than the mind, for those of us who are born of Africa. I came near to wishing that I had not chosen that moment to come back to this frontier of the Kalahari.

But then, suddenly, as we came over a neck between two hills and rounded a bend, a vast glimpse of the Kalahari itself lay open before us and, to my amazement, from the west to the northwest, a dark bank of thunderclouds, their crests silver and white with light and curling upwards like the greatest of Pacific rollers about to crash down on the sands of some encircled South Sea island, was already throwing its shadows over the horizon and reaching upwards to the sun itself. The sight was so totally unexpected that the impact of such a promise of rain was almost unbearable, akin to a kind of religious experience, and immediately I was invaded with a thought that seemed to threaten reason, posing the question that was almost its own answer as well: 'Dear God, could the witchdoctors be right after all?' And from there on my own quickening imagination felt totally inadequate to form any picture of what emotions this sight must produce among the Bakhatla.

By the time we got to the railway siding one peak of cloud, the Goodwin Austin or K2 of those Himalayas of thunder and lightning, was about to impinge on the lowering sun and I wondered if I would reach the capital before the rains broke, as I now had no doubt they would. I just hoped that the transport I had arranged with a European trader at Mochudi, who was an old friend, would be ready and waiting for me. As I bundled out of my carriage onto the dusty rails I saw, not far off, his Bakhatla storekeeper standing beside his 'Sutho pony, with a spare one bridled and saddled to hand. He appeared as relieved to see me as I was to see him.

We lost no time in mounting and setting off to Mochudi, an hour or so away on horseback. We rode fast, but soon the sun was lost behind the cloud, and, as the shadow of the clouds as well as the fall of day towards night diminished the light, we began to see an incessant play of lightning to the west and the northwest of us, sometimes sheet lightning which swept like the beams of a great lighthouse from behind the cloud, up and out into what was left of sky but, more and more often, sheer out of the heart of darkness of the storm itself, the long sword thrusts of stainless lightning – in which only Africa specializes – aimed straight at the earth. Then the voice of the storm would follow, profound, shaking the ground underneath our horses, and as it travelled the great desert corridors of silence and joined with other voices of thunder and rumbles from neighbouring clouds all was transformed into one of the greatest orchestrations of natural music of which so inspired a composer as the desert is capable. Hard on the music came the first astringent smell of the rain being welcomed with the rare fragrance of the gratitude of a patient, loving and forgiving earth.

I do not think I have ever enjoyed with such an acute ascent of excitement any ride across the veld of Africa as much as the ride from Palapye Road to Mochudi. In the process I became so identified and at one with the many dynamic elements of earth and sky moving into overwhelming harmony around me, that my feelings might have been those of some despatch rider on an immense battlefield sent out to solicit and bring back news to all the world of the storm and its significance. We were hardly in the trader's house, already shuttered against the storm, the massive oil lamp and candles lit, the mirrors covered with sheets and all silver and domestic metal wrapped in dishcloths and napkins by his Afrikaner wife, as essential prescriptions for warding off lightning, when the storm broke. A violent onslaught of wind, lightning now incessant, deafening thunder and, finally, the downpour of the heaviest of rain, and the atmosphere of relief and triumph over the defeat of one of the worst droughts ever known, removed all fear of what the storm could do to us in a house that suddenly seemed insignificant and frail. Indeed, the sound of the thunder and the rain on the galvanized iron roof became so great that we could hardly hear the conversation that followed our exchange of greetings. But words seemed never to have mattered less, so great was the feeling of celebration which took command in the storekeeper's house.

'Say what you like,' our host remarked in a shout which,

compared to the noise of the storm, was reduced almost to a whisper, 'those witchdoctors knew a thing or two.'

He had hardly spoken when there was a flash of lightning so close, white and fast that it seemed to dim our lamp and candlelight, and there was barely a second between it and the shock of sound that rocked our chairs. We did not know then, and only heard the story early the next morning, that it was the great fork of lightning which had demolished one of the huts crowded with close members of Molefi's family and killed seven of them.

But perhaps the most moving part of the occasion, which brought all those cosmic forces let loose in the world around us back into a specific focus, came when the music of the storm beat a slow, dignified and martial retreat towards the east and the violent downpour of rain settled into a steady fall which made the tenderest and most caring of refrains on the roof and earth around us, until suddenly we heard from without the sound of human voices. It was, however, a sound of voices I had never heard before, raised in a song full of an emotion of arrival as if it had travelled the world and was coming home. It came from a thousand men singing as only the Bantu can sing when their history rises in music sheer from deep in their stomachs where the human voice is born. They were singing the song of Molefi's impi, his own regiment, the trader told us. It was, he said, part of the age-old eve-of-inauguration ritual which demanded that, whenever a new chief was inaugurated, all the young men round about his own age were conscripted into a special battalion, armed with assegais, knobkerries and shields, to become responsible thereafter for his safekeeping to the end of his days; an equivalent, in fact, of our own royal household guards. The ritual demanded that, after nightfall on the eve of the inauguration, the chief alone with his regiment would move out in full battle formation to a secret place where they were met by the principal witchdoctor-priest for a special ceremony of initiation. There the chief-to-be would be inducted in the presence of so many witnesses that no doubters in the years to come could say that the induction had not been properly done. But there was, the trader had been told, at the climax of the initiation, a moment when the chief stepped out of the ring of warriors and went away into the night alone with the principal witchdoctor-priest. What was actually said and performed remained a secret between them. Outsiders, like ourselves, would know of the occasion only that it produced elemental song of the most strangely evocative kind, joined on this occasion to the drumming of thunder and the music of rain, all enclosed in the implications, without certainty or answer, of an intrusion of coincidence that then and now seemed to be at the least so extraordinary as to appear not of this world but its cosmos.

Long after the voice of the thunder had vanished, the music of the rain remained. I lay awake listening to it for hours and then even interrupted my sleep to sit up from time to time as if to reassure myself that what had happened was not imagined but really and joyfully true. It was not until an hour or so before dawn that the rain itself ceased and the whole mood of the world and the universe outside seemed to change from one of profound relief to an ascending atmosphere of jubilation, heightened, just before first light, by the sound of Molefi and his impi returning, singing with confirmation and affirmation in voices that reverberated as if it were one great voice alone. They passed by close enough to send a shiver through my room on the verandah, and I seemed to hear a constant reiteration, firmer and more positive with each repetition, proclaiming to one and all in those hushed huts like beehives on the hills around, something to the effect:

Yes, oh yes, yes. We have been there.
Yes. We have heard and we have seen.
Yes. It has been done.
Yes, oh yes, yes. All is well.

When, after breakfast, we walked to the tribal place of assembly in a bowl between hills covered with boulders of the oldest rock in the world, it was almost as if we could hear the grass and the bush regrowing and feel the quickening pulse of earth underneath our feet. Wherever we looked the land sparkled as if bejewelled, and the glimpses in between the clefts of the hills themselves revealed the country below, levelling out towards the immense desert in the west, flashing with pools and streams of water. The birds sang and called to one another as if they had never known thirst and famine, and the sky was of the purest and most feminine blue. Although we were early, the hills were already invested by thousands of women and young girls in their finest tribal jewellery and dress, and before we reached the central area the sound of birds and bubbling water was overcome by a hum of excitement coming from them as of bees swarming around their queen, busy building a labyrinthine palace of honey for her and their future.

When Molefi appeared, accompanied by Isang, both in totally incongruous European suitings, the inauguration ceremony was quickly accomplished and consisted of him standing in front of his chieftain's chair, Isang stepping forward to exchange some inaudible words and then tying an apron of burnished leopardskin around his throat and waist. The moment that was done, the women, from thousands of throats, raised their voices into one of the most stirring sounds I know. The word for it, unfortunately, does not do it justice and sounds more like an infection than the pure sound as of silver and crystal that it is. It is called ullulation; but by whatever name it is called, it went straight and unimpeded that morning up and out into the tranced blue as on winged sandals, carrying with it not only the spirit of gratitude and celebration induced by the rain in the Bakhatla, but also the hope and joy of renewal for the future invested in a handsome young boy.

The rest of the ceremony, had it not been for the women and their singing that had now set the blue a-trembling, would have been sheer anticlimax and contradiction. It began with a procession of men dancing, Isang at its head, throwing himself into the occasion with a heart and a determination great enough to prove to all that he harboured no resentment at his dispossession and was as loyally committed as anyone to the welfare of the boy who had taken his place. I had a feeling that for him it was a kind of prayer dance, since he knew better than anyone there the awesome burden of governing a black people at such a marginal moment in a land so marginally blessed as the Bakhatla's, and how they were already faced with the most momentous transition as of night into day, so starkly exemplified by the division between Molefi's initiation in the night before and his prosaic confirmation in the light which even so refreshed a morning could not exalt. What there was of dignity, for me, came not from the shy, hesitant young chief following in his uncle's steps but the way Isang led them, as if he had never known doubt or hesitation within, straight to a small church. And, of all churches, this one could not have been more remote from the pagan ceremony conducted the night before. It was a Dutch Reformed Church, perhaps one of the most Calvinistic institutions to be found in the world. There, to a reading of the Lord's Prayer, the Ten Commandments, a psalm of David, a long improvised sermon stuffed with moral prescriptions and the singing of hymns like, 'Now thank we all our God', Molefi's inauguration was fulfilled.

In the afternoon I went to call on Isang. I was alarmed to find that, whatever the coming of the rains may have done to ease the spirits of the Bakhatla, seeds of dissension had already been sown. Isang told me that all afternoon he had been beset by callers, ominously emphasizing to him that the rain had fallen not on the first day of Molefi's reign but on the last day of Isang's regency. They also hinted that, whichever way the matter was regarded, the omens were sombrely mixed, because what could you say of a portent like the storm when it eliminated by lightning seven of the new chief's closest relations? Was not this an indication that the witchdoctors had not read the will of the spirits with the accuracy expected of them?

I myself thought that this was going much too far; that, considering how many months had elapsed since the prophecy of rain was first uttered, no-one could have asked for greater precision. Isang smiled at me as if I were unduly naive and said that for him this reaction on the part of the tribe had great significance because it was a revelation of how seriously his people still took their witchdoctors, their vocation and role in the life of the nation.

He went on to tell me that he, of course, as was well known, disapproved totally of witchcraft. He regarded himself as a civilized and truly well educated person – educated at great tribal expense. Moreover, he was a Christian and had refused even to consider having more than one wife – and yet there was something about witchcraft still that made him wonder. He told me, for instance, that his first children were girls and that his wife came to him one day and said: 'Isang, I want to bear you a son. I am tired of having girls and you must do something about it.' He had told her he was doing all about it that a man could and, as he said that, laughed and explained: 'But you know what women are! She said that was not good enough. There was something I had not done yet. I should go and consult the chief witchdoctor.' He told me that he was extremely angry at that and could hardly speak to his wife for days. However, she nagged him so consistently and caused him so much trouble in his home that at last he went to see the witchdoctor. When he arrived, the witchdoctor was extremely rude to him, said that he knew why he had come, and told him to return to Mochudi, adding: 'And I will come when I come.'

Some weeks later the witchdoctor arrived. Once again he was extremely rude to Isang, ordered him to leave him alone with his wife and, when he emerged from their house, ignored Isang and went on his way. When Isang went indoors, his wife told him: 'This is what you have to do. You have to take the wood of a mopani tree and out of it carve the shape of a man child. You are to get a goat, kill it with your own hands, skin it, cure and tan the skin and make a shawl out of it. You are then to carry the wooden child in the shawl on your back wherever you go for seven days.'

Isang said that he was at once infuriated because these were all great indignities to pile on any man, let alone a chief. But in the days that followed his wife once more made his life so miserable that at last he consented to do what the witchdoctor had ordered. And then – I still remember the voice and the tone in which he told me this, some sixty-five years ago, oracular with all the enigmas and unpredictability of the future enclosed within it – he continued in a hushed voice: 'And you know, the next child was a boy. Now you can dismiss this purely as an idle coincidence, but you know, after that my wife had two more girls. As a result she came to me and demanded that

109

I should go through the whole, humiliating process again so that she could have another boy. Well, you know what women are. In the end I had to give way and, would you believe it, the next child again was a boy. Now, what the hell do you make of that?' As he finished he slapped his thigh, which I remember scattered all the flies gathered around the edges of a white beaded doily over the jug of milk on the table beside him.

We followed this with a long discussion of the 'Sutho tribes in Bechuanaland, as it was then called, and of the past and present of the Bakhatla in particular. In the process Isang seemed to become another kind of person, some kind of trustee of his people's spirit. I felt this so strongly that I asked him about the ceremony the night before and in particular what happened between Molefi and the witch-doctor. He could only tell me of his own experience as one of the impi formed for the inauguration of Molefi's father – his own immediate elder brother. All they knew was that it had to do with the secret of the soul of their tribe which from then on was held to be singularly in the chief's keeping. It was a sacred secret and went back to the days when the First Spirit spoke to a plenipotentiary of the 'Sutho people in a cave in hills on the far, far marches of Barotseland, still the ancestral and spiritual home of true 'Sutho peoples.

He took me then for a final walk to see the sun going down, with the light already gold, and as of an emanation of forgiveness from the darkening heaven for what it had done to the earth before the coming of the rain. We watched it from a cave set in a hill behind the bowl where the inauguration had taken place. It was a cave wherein his grandfather, the great Linchwe, who was a kind of chief and seer combined, had gone to meditate for days on end and, it was believed, spoke to the great, wise old serpent

110

which commanded the rains and somewhere encircled the world of their beginnings. Linchwe, he said, had guarded the secret and protected their soul as no-one in their history had done. On this evening he wanted us to watch the fateful day end there, I felt, as a sign of supplication to Linchwe's spirit to ensure that the secret would not be lost in the days to come.

All this made us silent and we sat still, watching a sky for once clear of dust and the long, level light of evening brushing the far Kalahari as if with archangelic wings bound on a mission of benediction, the peak of another range of cloud impinging over the rim of the sun. There were, it warned us, more storms to come, but I knew of no place where such storms would be more welcome to the earth. But what of the mind and soul of the Bakhatla? And what of the secret once so meditated and rehearsed in the cave behind us? I looked at Isang and knew I could not ask him, because if ever a heart had trouble enough the expression on his face suggested he had. When the gold went from the sky and the sky went brown, bats upside down in their holes behind us turned upright and launched themselves swifter even than swifts on the air; the land below went black, without light of even a solitary fire, and we were back, it seemed, in an hour before man and his word. The whole mood of the evening suddenly changed. Isang too had taken it as a sign to go. Yet he rose reluctantly from his seat of stone, and as we walked back, with the night plover piping as a bosun might pipe his ship home from the sea, we hardly spoke. The visit to the cave somehow had said it all. But in the west lightning hurled from below the horizon began to dim the stars, and spoke of storm to come.

At the time I had felt as on my first visit to the Kalahari, that all that had gone before – witchdoctors, storm and now Isang and myself — were being remembered by the great memory of which I have spoken. I have thought of it again and again over the long years that have followed and wondered what happened to the secret and to the soul of the people it was designed to promote. Molefi, handsome, intelligent and plausible as he was, was corrupted by his power, served his people badly and died an alcoholic. And, over the years, the grip of a barbarous technological revolution holds not only the Bakhatla but all the Kalahari more and more firmly in its cast-iron fist. Looked at selfishly, however, the experience served me well. It was another rung down a long ladder of mind and spirit to a meeting in a basement of time with the first people of my native country where they appeared almost as the great memory itself made flesh.

Yet, for all these experiences, this compulsive interest in the Kalahari did not bring about my encounter with its undiscovered heartland, which consisted of the greater part of its 250,000 square miles, until many years later. The how and the why of it has been dealt with in *The Lost World of the Kalahari*, and the consequences in a sequel called *The Heart of the Hunter*. The aboriginal role of the desert itself in my life, however, was not relevant enough to be recounted, yet it figured prominently in the background of those four years, in the beginning of the fifties, when I spent from three to four months every year, and once nearly six months, in exploring the great unknown between the well-established routes across the Kalahari. In a series of systematic zig-zags I travelled from the Zambezi to the Molopo and from the foothills of the great inner plateau of Africa on the frontiers of the Transvaal and Botswana to its border in South West Africa. I made time, even, for probes into South West Africa and Angola up to Mossamedes, because the Kalahari is not confined to

Botswana but overflows its borders in the west and north and fills the profound rift in the earth which begins at Lake Baikal in Siberia, passes through central Asia, Jordan, the Dead and Red Seas, on south to end in the northern districts of the Cape of Good Hope, under thick vegetable cover from the Orange to the Congo river.

Some of the results of what I saw and felt are described in official papers to the Colonial Office, and one memorable expedition is recorded in a book called *Kalahari Sands*, by Professor Frank Debenham, who was the official geologist of Scott on his last journey to the Antarctic. There was also a special mission headed by that remarkable public servant who successfully managed the great cotton experiment launched by the British Government in the Gazirah of the Sudan, Arthur Gaitskell, the elder brother of Hugh, leader of the Labour Party who, alas, died too young to fulfil the promise that was so obviously entrusted to his nature. This last mission, which Arthur Gaitskell chaired but which I led, still had a dream of establishing a cattle industry in the crownlands of the Kalahari for the benefit of the impoverished 'Sutho peoples inhabiting a country with hardly any known natural resources. Although I briefly joined in the vision, what I subsequently saw of the lot of the Bushman, and experienced of the animal and plant life of the central desert and along the west and northern fringes of the Kalahari, made me change my mind and I did nothing to promote it.

But memorable as was my encounter in the central desert with Bushmen still living their stone-age way, in exploring so great a physical unknown what mattered most, perhaps, was the fact that I was exploring a great unknown area within my own spirit or, to put it in the idiom with which I began, re-remembering the great memory with which I had been in danger of losing a contact I needed for my

113

own renewal. The unknown without inevitably led to the unknown within, and in the process consolidated the emancipation of myself from nearly a decade of war. In spite of the fact that those years in the fifties meant that I was separated from people I dearly loved and had only just rejoined after the long separation imposed by the war, I do not think I have ever known happier or more meaningful years. I could never have imagined that just the act of breaking through into new desert country without man-made roads or even tracks, knowing that it was land which no human eyes, except perhaps Bushman eyes, had seen, would create a feeling of fulfilment which nothing else had ever given me in so powerful an ascending measure. Moreover, this land itself seemed to respond equally to my presence as if it had long wanted to have contact with some form of humanity.

I came out with my trucks, for instance, in the far north as we broke through dense mopani, stormwood, mahogany, fever tree and ironwood belts back onto the grass veld, struggled over a ridge and down into a pan, round as a ripple on a still pond, and found it covered with animals of all kinds – eland, gemsbock, springbuck, hartebeest, tsessebee and even a kudu of an exceptional stature. The animals made no attempt whatsoever to scatter and run away but made way for us slowly and with dignity, looking at us first with total amazement and then with expressions of distaste for the noise of our engines and smell of their exhausts, snorting as if to blow so unwholesome an incense from their nostrils and twitching their ears and shaking their heads at such pollution of silence and air. At several holes, silver-backed and bat-eared jackals darted out, and even a lone hyena on the rim of the pan stood trembling on stretched-out legs as if in danger of falling over with the shock of surprise and urge to question the nature of so rude a disturbance and express his disapproval of our lack of desert manners. Although we made camp at the far edge of the pan in the early afternoon and stayed there all night long, the animals remained by their salt licks until our departure the next day. At one moment in the night I woke up from my position well away from the main camp, because I liked to be alone and free of any sounds of sleeping to enjoy a sky sagging under its weight of stars, where I could feel clearly whatever the music of the night suggested, or welled up from this accelerating process of re-remembering within myself, and found that the animals had grouped themselves around us so near that I could almost touch them with my hand. I wondered at such a state of innocence, and thought of the Garden at our beginning before our Fall, and the wonder was heightened when the noises on the far side of the pan told me they had come to us because of an instinct that there was protection having us as neighbours against the hunters of the night, coughing and snorting beyond the sandy ridges of their pan.

I had, from the beginning, made a point of naming each camp. The feeling that we were leaving behind something of our perishable selves that ought to be remembered when we had gone, made me go out and carve on the most suitable trunk a smooth white blaze, and engrave in the blaze a name for the place and fill in the lettering with indelible pencilling, hoping that 'indelible' was more than a commercial euphemism. This camp had impressed my companions so much that Frank Debenham insisted on our calling it 'Paradise Pan'.

And then the land itself was full of reminders that it was no longer what it had once been and that it, too, like all things mortal, despite its apparent invincibility in its manifestations of sand and stone against the wear and tear of time and change, had been transformed into something

115

which its appearance could no longer express but could convey only in an atmosphere of a brooding sort of nostalgia, so dense that at its climaxes in the light of dawn and fall of night I thought of it as a mood of irreparable loss. It became clear to me, for instance, that from the north to the south, as I learnt more of its system of pans and dry riverbeds – all these depressions and courses increasing in depth, so that I would travel along beds that were still hard with primeval clay for days on end down and on between canyons of sand, becoming deeper and more monumental the further south we went – that they must once have been immense watercourses filled to the brim with flowing water. Judging by what I knew of the Okavango delta, and discovered of Lake Ngami and the Makarikari, they were once part of a vast, natural spread of water linked to rivers with their source in the mountains and the rains of the far interior of Angola, and it was as if this land, too, was in the grip of its own sense of exile from a Garden state, fed by ample waters, like that of our own mythological beginning.

So day and night we breathed and moved as if wrapped in a mystery that did not produce mystification of faculties but such a vision of the past and expectation of the future that all seemed but beginning without end. All the complex of experiences of which these are only a few examples, with their imponderables weightier even than the tangible, transformed mystery into wonder, making a mood of reverence for all we saw and felt with a rare humility that I assume is what is meant by religious experience.

And what seemed to be most significant to me in the progression over the days and the repetition over the years of this experience of the desert, was how always, as our time went by, the men with me would start talking as if surprised by the fact that they found themselves dreaming as they had never before dreamed. They suddenly began, one after the other, to talk of their dreams as if they had only just discovered the process, sitting there over coffee around our fire and waiting for the red dawn to break: the Heitse-Eibib dawn, as the Hottentots called it, after their god who returned wounded and bleeding from another victorious battle against the forces of darkness in the night.

Frank Debenham, who was a dear, imaginative, sensitive and feeling human being of a kind that the harsh land of Australia has a gift for breeding, had a series of dreams which was perhaps most revealing of all, with a certain objective interest that our other dreams did not possess. Debenham had never again experienced anything in life that had so profound an impact on him as his two years in the Antarctic with Scott's expedition. He had made particular friends of Bill Wilson and Birdie Bowers then, and still talked of his own hurt when both perished within a few miles of the safety of the base where Debenham and the rest of the expedition were anxiously waiting. Debenham, as the journey in the Kalahari went on, would recall those days more and more frequently, so much so that I composed a sort of Alice in Wonderland poem about him which, alas, I can no longer remember but was to the effect that we had to thank God for Captain Scott who took 'Debby' to a place so cold that he would have to fall in love later with another so hot as the Kalahari. What lay between 'Scott' to make it rhyme with 'hot' has gone with the wind and dust of that journey. But some fragments of his recollections remain clearly.

For instance, Debenham would often re-insist, as if answering an invisible ring of soft-cushioned critics around our fire, that the essence of Scott and the spirit induced by him in those who accompanied him could be summed up in the way they died. Although Scott's diaries make it clear that they had the means with them for taking their own lives, when they found themselves enclosed for the last time in the last fatal blizzard and knew they were going to perish, they decided unanimously to die naturally. He would speak also, as if it were the main ingredient of an Aeschylean drama, of Scott's error which, he thought, made tragedy inevitable. This was Scott's decision to add Petty-Officer Evans to the polar party, raising the number from six to seven, even though all the sledges and their provisions had been made up for a group of only six, and introducing an asymmetrical factor into their journey that slowed them down enough to fail within barely a score of miles from their base. Scott had done this, he would emphasize to his listeners, whom his words had transported from hot and breathless sands to the ice of the Antarctic, out of his loyalty and regard for an old shipmate, but Fate, with its awesome responsibility for administering the enigmatic justice of the universe with ruthless impartiality, punished this breach of law by making Evans, who was first to crack physically, the instrument of the ultimate tragedy.

Debenham would describe how, with Apsley Cherry-Garrard, who wrote the classic *The Worst Journey in the World*, he had been of the party which went to look for Scott when the spring came. They found them frozen, but at peace, as if forever asleep in their little tent. What struck him above all was how, not dead, but strangely alive Bill Wilson looked. And ever since then, he said, he had a dream which came to him from time to time, on each occasion more convincing than the last.

In that dream he would find himself walking past a Georgian terrace in Sydney, down a green slope towards the waterfront and, as he neared it, seeing two people come out of the sea and start up towards him. To his amazement, he discovered they were Wilson and Bowers, more alive even than they were when living. He would ask Wilson in amazement: 'But where have you been all this time?' and Wilson would answer to the effect that, well, it was quite simple: when the polar journey was ended they just walked into the sea, right down to the bottom and walked along its floor until they came to the waterfront at Sydney and, well, there they were! Debenham would wake up with a great sense of wonder and joy, and amazed that he himself had never thought of anything so simple. But never before, he stressed, had this dream come to him so often and so insistently as on this journey in the Kalahari.

Then on his last night in the Kalahari at a camp whose name was carved into a great camelthorn tree, which had become the archetypal tree of Kalahari life to me, as 'Debenham's Rest', he had another dream which seemed to mean even more to him than the one I have just recounted. Like all meaningful dreams, it was simple. He dreamt that he saw me walking towards him and holding out what looked like a magazine between my hands for him to see. And as I handed it to him, to his amazement it was just a magazine called 'LIFE' in large, shining letters, and below it a noble white horse ready for mounting. And I wondered then, as I often wonder in almost total recall of the occasion, how much the night that preceded it had contributed to what seemed to me, amateur as I am in these things, so vital a dream.

I always made camp early in the Kalahari so that we could have enough daylight to prepare ourselves for the night, but on this occasion the ideal site I wanted for our last camp had presented itself earlier than usual. The choice was made imperative by the appearance, almost in direct line of our compass bearing, of one of the tallest dead trees, still upright despite the rot in its veins, that I have ever seen. Since we were now in the southernmost Kalahari it

stood, white as a skeleton, in a kind of glade with a surround of the finest camelthorn trees. They were so sturdy
and healthy and their umbrella of leaves so green and thick
that it made the skeleton tree disturbingly haunting, even
in that clear light of an evening of pure gold. Yet, despite
its ghostly appearance, my imagination seized on it with
joy because on all the last nights I have ever had in the
desert since my boyhood I had pitched my camp around
equivalents of such a tree so that, when the darkness fell, I
could make our fire around its base, set it alight and settle
ourselves for the last meal, under a Kalahari sky, trembling
with the clearest of stars, tiptoe on the leaves above us.

I should, perhaps, from all that the Bushmen had taught
me of fire, have had a feeling of guilt in preparing to make
so unusually big a fire, judged even by my own valedictory
practices. They themselves in spirit were still so near to the
moment when their god-hero, the praying mantis, had given
them the gift of fire by stealing it from under the wing of
the ostrich, that it was still miraculous to them. Although
dry wood was abundant in the desert, as a source of fire it
was treated with the utmost reverence. Their little fires were
always small, and their flame precise and pointed like the
tip of one of their arrows. All my memories of nights with
groups of stone-age hunters in the desert were clearly held
in the focus of fire that was still sacred to man, surrounded
by ancient stone-age faces and apricot bodies, satin with
flame, an echo as of sound at the end of a tunnel of their
voices and the click of their consonants, crackling like electricity on their lips, joining in the crackle of the burning
wood.

Whenever they visited me in my own camp they were
astonished and somewhat outraged by the size of my own
fire, and would rebuke me for so wasteful a use of wood.
I was never to know what they would have said of so great

a display of fire as in any of my last camps because when that occurred I had always left stone-age Bushman, alas, a long way behind, but it was not difficult to imagine that they would have found it inexcusable, even as the solemn gesture of farewell I meant it to be. However, the occasion was always redeemed for me by the fact that the mood induced by these fires was invariably full of respect and reverence and gratitude for what the desert had given us.

I would justify my breach of good Bushman law by recalling how in our European beginnings many cultures cremated their dead and burnt their belongings with the bodies, because through the fire they believed they freed the imperishable spirit from the perishable substances in which it had been clothed for its brief appearance on the stage of the here and now, and so ensured that all they had found of imperishable meaning through their possessions would be freed to accompany them on their journey into the beyond. It was, perhaps, I would tell myself, a similar instinct, with which our culture had long since lost conscious contact, that had made us choose a source of fire large enough to ensure that what had been imperishable in the journey behind us would be freed to accompany us back into the world from which we had come. The camelthorn trees which we could see dimly beyond the frontiers of light cast by this tree on fire were images in the night of the tree of immediate life. This tree of fire around which we had our last meal seemed the basic image of fire that burnt on even when we and the tree itself were burnt out. Certainly, the shape itself expressed some such aspiration, if not fulfilment, of meaning because there was a moment that night at Debenham's Rest when the flames reached the summit of the dead tree, and so still was it that the whole fire from base to its spear-pointed tip seemed deprived of movement and stood there, motionless, in the dark like the

121

spire of a great Gothic cathedral in flame. Even the silence of the desert, which was always a rustle of all the delicate sound suppressed by the rough day, stood still and opened, as it were, the windows of the night to let in the whisper of the coals feeding the flame from within the fire itself, making it kin to the 'still small voice' described in the Old Testament as the intimation of the transfiguration of death into life in the heart of a prophet as he sat alone on the rim of a desert in Palestine.

The expressions on the faces of my companions on that last night were so at one that I marvelled at it, because their differences of character and upbringing could not have been greater and their points of origin more remote from one another. In every roll-call that I have held in the many recollections of the occasion, this extraordinary sense of resolution remains dominant. The cowboy from New Mexico, Jack Games, Frank Debenham from Australia, Cyril Challis from a suburb of London, and Brian Currie from the house of the owner of a coalmine in Stafford by way of the trenches and the Northern Frontier District of Kenya; Johnny Marnewick, my guide, who had been born in an oasis in the Kalahari and whose fastidious memory of a journey after exceptional rains across the Kalahari with his father at the age of seven made us find a source of water long dismissed as a desert myth; and Harry Bennett, my Irish mechanic, whose inspired way with broken engines did not diminish the quality of his romantic tenor that sang songs to us, sheer out of the great Celtic twilight which will not yet set into night, so eloquently that even the lion were silent with envy of so rounded a sound; myself from a village in the interior, and John Mosuothwane from a kraal on the borders of Matabeleland, and the rest of our company, all lost our map references and were possessed by a sense of having the same point of departure, and the same pattern of return to where origin and destination are one. Somehow Debenham's dream as well as our assembly at first light and the mood after his recital of the dream suggest that this reading of something impossible to describe was still also dealing, however subjectively, with something objective.

This something objective, after Debenham's account of the dream, seemed so important that I did not want the usual breakfast, the conversation and the bustle of breaking camp to take it away from me. I left the task of dismantling our home for the night to my guide, took my gun and military compass and walked off alone into the desert in the direction we had to take. It caused no surprise among my companions because it was something I always loved to do. It enabled me to read the spoor of animals and birds in the sand as one might a diary of all that had happened in the night. Especially I could listen in, uninterrupted, to the song of the birds. This urge was a significant example of how the longer one was part of the desert, the more some ancient, forgotten aspect in oneself was resurrected and daily became increasingly active, so that one found portents in the behaviour of the natural life around one, as some Odyssean wanderer did in the blind days of Homer. Something in one would read it as if it were one's daily newspaper, weather forecast and all, and never more so than in the liquid vocabulary of birds, particularly at nightfall and early morning; so that, for me, there was a precious quality in their rendering of their song, which contained, however vaguely, a premonition of what kind of a day there was to come, and which made it clear why it had made them such a preferred source of omens in the oracular, far past, and, far as it was behind us, brought it near.

Then there was also a private and personal consideration: as always, the knowledge that it was my last day in the desert had depressed me inordinately. Whatever natural joy my return to my own world and people I loved would give me, at that particular moment it did not prevent me from feeling like someone condemned to say farewell to freedom and to return to prison.

As it happened, it was another morning of singular purity and harmony within itself and all that encompassed it. I walked some four miles before the recollection that I might be going too far and too fast stopped me. The hour and a half it had taken me, because of my total participation in this state of natural intercommunication, seemed very much less. Only the ridge of a pan rising above the level earth not far ahead of me stopped me from going on, and its silhouettes of trees of thorn on the rim broke in on me with the realization that I knew the place. Almost proudly, because I felt that the act of recognition was so immediate and aboriginal, I went towards it like an honorary native of the desert. Quickly I climbed the rim and confirmed that it was indeed a pan I had not only visited before but camped in. The feeling of knowing it and being known to it made it a memorable arrival, as if I had just arrived in the desert equivalent of another town, which the best of inhabited pans always made me feel. At that hour, however, there were few of its citizens about. On the edge only a few lingering gazelle in the glass of morning, like a reflection rather than their substantial selves, were setting out for their business in bush and brush beyond. Two large groups of meerkats were spreading out from their ghetto basements along the edge of the pan. Already some of their sentinels were on point duty to the north and south, upright and alert, one on a termite mound, another on the rim itself and a third on top of a dead tree, his head still as on a statue of himself, while he watched a marshall eagle rising on a spiral of air dangerously near. I could never look at meerkats without a feeling of the sheer fun of being alive reborn in me, and the reaffirmed gift of their affection for one another and joy in each other's company that sets their little kibbutzes apart from all other animal congregations, quickening an awareness of the love involved in the act and deed of nature, however disguised in the ruthless aspects enforced by its commitment to survival. They were constantly pausing to see if their friends were near, or turning about just to touch someone special with a tender and caring paw. At intervals I could hear bursts of their singsong little voices which chant good-morning and croon lullabies to one another at night and even maintain their musical quality when they warn one another at the top of their scale that some bateleur eagle or lamb-snatcher is moving close to strike. Between me and them, a tall secretary bird, with the stride of a born civil servant, was advancing towards the centre of the pan as if to his town clerk's office. Marching proudly right across the centre, a lone old male ostrich went, booming as if he were the town crier himself, but almost immediately the sound was lost to me in the far-off drone of my trucks setting out towards me. We were travelling through country where the going was so heavy that we were happy if we covered twenty miles a day. I knew it would be an hour or so before the trucks would reach me, yet it says so much for the quality of the silence and its counterpoint of melodious animal and bird sound that I heard them as if they were only on the other side of the pan.

I turned about to where, in the east, the day was still fresh and the sun had had as yet no time to blur the light of day by melting it into something like liquid glass which distorted and blurred high noon until the physical world presented itself in images which came near to making one feel the subject of intense hallucination. In that light, still

125

blue with the shadow in their laps, rose the hills on the frontier beyond Lobatsi. For some months one's eyes had become accustomed to a world that was almost always flat and, when not flat, troubled only by the rhythmical outline of symmetrical dunes as a mariner's view is cradled between waves of freshening breeze of the level ocean before him.

I was not prepared for what those hills did to me then. A rush of totally unforeseen emotion rose up like a gush of deep artesian water within me. I found myself close to tears and remembered, as if the memory recalled the emotion itself of the creator in the act of raising those hills above the earth. For the first time, I believe, the full impact of the psalmist's 'I will lift mine eyes unto the hills from whence cometh my help' reached me.

I stood there staring at them for a while, in a state of prayer without words, before I reluctantly turned about and walked back until I could see my leading truck breaking through the bush and the grass. So plentiful had been the rains that year, and the response of the earth so generous, that my little convoy travelled towards me encircled in a halo of gold from the mist of pollen dislodged in tasselled grass and beflowered brush.

The first thing I did when we arrived back at the pan was to take Frank Debenham on to the ridge and point him also towards the east. The pan now was empty, the town crier had gone as well as the gazelles, and elsewhere all the plants and birds and animals were out of sight, but the light was not yet distorted and the hills still wore some shadow around their crowns. I did not speak but watched Debenham. At once, I could tell that he was experiencing a similar emotion. When he turned to look at me again there were tears in his eyes. I knew then that the emotion in him must have been even more powerful than it was in me. I knew that I could return again to that place and that state, provided I earned the right, by another desert search behind me. He knew that his was both the first and last, and the meaning of his dream, perhaps, that his horse, as it were, was waiting, and he must remount and ride on.

When I had written *The Lost World of the Kalahari* and done the television series, I secured what I thought would be a lasting voice for the Bushmen in our administration of their desert affairs. For the first time in history, a sympathetic Colonial Office and an exceptional Provincial Commissioner, who was the Resident at the time, appointed an officer charged singularly as a trustee of Bushman welfare. Part of his brief was to live with them, study their language and their ways, and learn not only of their physical but their inner needs which made them so special to an age standing with its back so resolutely turned on its origin as ours. I thought that, with such a beginning, a dignified future for the Bushman could evolve. The awareness of their plight, which I had helped to create through television programmes that were shown all over the world and has the most heartening response from ordinary people, as well as the two books I had written to give it a more permanent and lasting reality, I hoped would produce a new climate of spirit that would consolidate and enlarge a hard-won bridgehead in the imperviousness, the greed and corruption by power of both black and white cultures which had come so near to extinguishing the Bushman altogether.

Meanwhile I worked in other ways in whatever leisure moments I had throughout the years to encourage the welfare of all the peoples who shared this great world with the Bushman. I spent many days with John Maud when he was preparing himself for the task of High Commissioner in southern Africa. I found him an imaginative source for following through some of the conclusions which my own experiences of that world had imposed upon me. For instance, in the immediate political dimension, I persuaded him of the urgency of removing the seat of the government of Botswana from Mafeking in the Union of South Africa to Gaborone, where it now is. I had already thought for years how absurd it was that the British Protectorate of Bechuanaland should still be administered from what was called the 'Imperial Camp' in Mafeking, some forty miles across the border in the Union of South Africa. This sense of the absurdity and wastefulness of such an administrative anachronism was joined by the distaste with which I viewed the proclamation of the apartheid doctrine in South Africa and its accelerating political and social promotion.

I had come back not long before my meeting with John Maud from an expedition on which I had conducted a Royal Commission of which I was a member and which included Bathoein of the Bamangkwetse, and Tsekedi Khama of the Bamangwato, two of the great chiefs in a country which had a long history of stable and gifted chief-tainship. It was my first meeting with Bathoein, who has since become a close friend – and happily is still alive and still plays the organ in his church – but not with Tsekedi Khama. I had known him since he first appeared in the Cape as a young man of barely twenty, newly appointed to be a regent of his tribe and guardian over the son of his brother, who had been assassinated. I took a great liking to him and warmed to his mission of testing in law the validity of mineral concessions which he felt had been unfairly exacted from his people when gold and diamond fever swept all over southern Africa from the 1880s onwards. I had been able to help him and his advocate, whom I knew well, to elicit newspaper support for his mission. The two of them readily joined our group – an American Professor of Animal Husbandry, Brian Currie (an old friend of mine from Kenya and companion on many previous expeditions), Arthur Gaitskell and myself. In the course of the journey through the deep Kalahari which our work on the Royal Commission demanded of us, we came to a small oasis where a white merchant and storekeeper, born in South Africa, provided the link between a tribe of Bakhgalakadi and the outside world.

We arrived there just before lunch and were promptly invited to eat with the storekeeper. From what I had seen of him in that short while, and his attitude to the people in his store, I saw nothing but trouble in the invitation. I took Arthur Gaitskell, our chairman, on one side, begged him to say no to the lunch and to move on at once. I was just beginning to explain to him why, because my attitude puzzled him, when the storekeeper joined us and I had to desist. The lunch accordingly was arranged as I feared it would be arranged, and out of this fear had excused myself on the grounds that I was not hungry and would be happy later to call for a cup of tea in the kitchen. When, soon after, lunch was on the table, Gaitskell and the European members of our mission were taken to the dining room, and these two 'Sutho aristocrats, Bathoein and Tsekedi, conducted to a table without cloth in the kitchen, where I went to join them. The fact that this form of apartheid was still possible and practised, even in a country of indigenous people under British Protection, seemed to me part of a state of mind and values which diminished the dignity and reduced the moral authority of an officialdom clinging to their Imperial Camp in Mafeking.

Moreover, when we re-emerged from the Kalahari and arrived in Mafeking to see the Provincial Commissioner in charge of the Protectorate, he invited the Commission to dinner at Dixons Hotel in Mafeking. Again I refused, for the same reason as I had refused at the trader's store in the Kalahari, because I knew that Tsekedi and Bathoein would never be admitted in Dixons Hotel, or that, if they were, there would be an instant riot in the town that night. So I let the rest of the members of the Commission have their meal at Dixons, and organized a meal for Tsekedi and Bathoein and myself in the house of a friend. Nothing could have demonstrated more clearly how far Mafeking values had infiltrated the Imperial Camp spirit, that its Chief Officer found nothing reprehensible in organizing such a selective dinner. Whatever arguments colonial bureaucracy may have produced against removal of the capital of the Protectorate from where it had been for generations of the imperial day, these sorts of examples seemed to John Maud, as they did to me, as unanswerable as they were dangerous, and in due course a new capital was created well within Botswana at Gaborone.

Then I also went with him in detail into what should be done about the cattle industry of Botswana. I had already helped to launch two successful cattle-ranching pilot schemes, one of which is today fully matured, greatly expanded and successful, and urged the continuing import-ance of abattoirs to the peasant cattlemen, on the lines of the one in whose establishment at Lobatsi I had played a part – incidentally, something so practical I had thought it might have been a counter against the charge of being some confused mixture of the mystical and romantic which, even in those days, rationalists and materialists brought against me, spelling mystic in their hearts not with a 'y' but an 'i', making it of the mist and not of the myth.

These are just some samples of the ingredients of a total vision, as I saw it, which I shared with him to such an extent that quite a bit of Harold Macmillan's famous 'winds of change' speech to the startled South African Parliament, as well as the title itself, was conceived in my home in London. That done, I felt I had earned my discharge from the contract that this strange desert had imposed on me from birth. In that belief I had tried to carry on my own work from where it had been interrupted by the outbreak of war, but those years of expiation, as I called them to myself, which followed it, seemed to have redeemed my bond. As a result, I did not go back to the Kalahari until some thirty-five years after that last goodbye to it, in spite of the fact that it haunted me not only on certain evocative days but regularly in dreams, from which I would wake with a longing to return to it, like an ache in my physical being.

When I did return again, the ostensible purpose was to help in the making of another television film, *Testament to the Bushmen*, which would record how they had fared after my sojourn among them in the central desert more than a generation before. What I saw then was shattering. Whatever I might have hoped to have achieved for their protection and the promotion of their culture had proved utterly vain. How and why this happened after the safeguards I have described is a whole and another story, although the overall theme is implied clearly in all I have written. The fact was that stone-age man as I had known him had vanished since I had last been there, and the pathetic remnants we found no longer lived in their traditional way, though the memory of it was still so near and dear to them that they acted it out for the cameras with a great relish and conviction.

I was filled with despair and apprehension at this evidence that the arrogance and imperviousness of a culture based on the Jacob values of life, as I labelled its concentration on husbandry, personal possessions, manufacture and all sorts of shallow economic preconceptions, was the same slanted and specialized spirit which had caused the elimination of the Bushman's ancestors – who had committed themselves as purely to the care and nourishment of nature as a salmon to the sea, and found nature far kinder and more compassionate than the black and white invaders of their land. The apprehension was all the greater because by now I realized it was just another facet of a worldwide unawareness in modern man and a measure of the alarming narrowing of his consciousness which increasingly was divorcing our time from our natural sources of energy and direction, and impoverishing our societies and the meaning of life itself for the first time everywhere in the world simultaneously.

I remembered how often the Bushman I knew in the central desert had come to seem to me rich in a way in which we were poor, and how they moved, though practically naked, clothed and vivid in their own immediate experience and apprehension of life. Wherever they went, they seemed to feel themselves not as strangers but known in a way in which we have long ceased to feel known, and accordingly we have so lost an inner sense of belonging that, in my own case, after a war produced by our alienation from what was natural in ourselves, I had to go back to the bush of Africa and the desert to help me towards rediscovering it.

All this came to a particular point at a visit to the Tsodilo Hills, the 'Slippery Hills', where I had the experience which is described in detail in *The Lost World of the Kalahari*. I started this probe from a place on the Okavango River where I had done my own journey into the swamp itself. Already the earth there was proclaiming its own desperation and alarm. The ample riverene forest on the fringes of the river, and its great delta gleaming wide and far like a piece of jewellery of precious stones cast away on the sands of the desert, seemed to me to have contracted so much that it was only an embattled line of trees along the banks of the river itself.

The Tsodilo Hills, which I had discovered, or perhaps rediscovered, for European man, were by now so well known that there were several roads to it and even a landing strip at the hills themselves to make them accessible to the increasing numbers of tourists, induced in the first instance, I fear, by my films and books into wanting to see them. I myself, because of pressure of time, landed there on an airstrip large enough to take sizeable aeroplanes, and found two other planes already drawn up at the side waiting for their cargo of tourists to return from the hills where they had been to look at the most accessible rock-paintings for a few hours on their way to somewhere else.

Only one incident redeemed the visit from the arid platitude it has become for the world of today, to give me back some of the original sense of wonder and special meaning with which those hills had once invested me, and that was a coincidence too remarkable to be misunderstood. As I walked from the plane to the edge of the landing strip I saw two black men coming through the surrounding bush towards us. When they came nearer I thought I knew one of them, but this seemed so unlikely that I dismissed it until one man began to wave his hand at me in an excited manner and suddenly I saw that it was Samutchao who, with his father Samutchoso, had been one of my guides on my first expedition to the hills. At that time he was a young fisherman and breeder of cattle and goats along the Okavango River, but now he had moved out and organized himself and a whole community of Makoba clansmen around water found for them by the government of Botswana, close to the hills – which at the same time had enabled it to dispossess the Bushman of yet more of his vital and shrinking hunting grounds. Samutchao had obviously become the

133

most important person in the area and a person of power, which I was to find had not improved him. However, he went gladly back with me and my companions into the hills.

Together we retraced the journey to the first rock-painting I had discovered, one hot summer's morning, glowing on yellow sandstone above the thorn trees. We climbed up to the ledge underneath the paintings themselves where I had buried in an empty bottle of Plymouth Gin the letter I had written to the spirits of the hills, begging their pardon for the irreverence of our intrusion and our inconsiderate behaviour on our arrival. The ledge had greatly diminished over those long years. The earth which had covered the bottle had been eroded by rain and sun and wind, and the bottle and the letter, I was to discover, had been lodged in the government museum in the capital of Botswana.

We retraced also the journey we had done from the base below the paintings, up to the bowl on top where the master spirits of all the animals created for life in the Kalahari had left their footprints in the slabs of rock, indelible even under such extremes of sun and weather. We rediscovered the marks in the stone where the Great First Spirit had knelt to ask creation for a blessing on his work. Then, the holes within were clearcut and clean, but now, through lack of human care and devotion, they were filled with sand. Samutchao on that first occasion had knelt on the rocks and himself prayed to the spirit and, happily, was caught in that attitude on our camera in a way which still testifies to the relationship there was then between man, beast, bird, plant and earth. But this time he walked past without noticing. I had to call him back to verify that this indeed was the sacred spot. I reminded him of what he had done on my last visit. He gave me a rather wan smile of recollection but did not repeat his act of prayer.

The pool of everlasting water we found dry and empty. The tree bearing the fruit of the knowledge of good and evil, of which the book speaks, had gone. I asked Samut-chao what had happened to the water, and the question broke through his indifference. His nonchalant body became violent as it were with new life, and he waved both his arms at the pit empty of water and almost shouted: 'All gone, gone, gone! All gone with the spirits back into the earth where they came from.'

And I remembered how already, thirty-five years before, on the morning when we had climbed up to offer our letter of contrition to the spirits and the white-haired Samutchoso – whose name meant 'He who was left after the reaping' – having consulted the spirits in the manner I described, turned to me and, with a voice of unbelievable sadness, remarked even then: 'You know, Moren, the spirits are not what they were. They are losing their power. Even ten years ago they would have killed us for what we have done.' The expression on his face then was charged with an archaic sense of tragic and Teiresian foreboding of doom.

Going down from the hills we met a Bushman, in every physical way a classical example of what the pure aboriginal Bushman was like, not setting out on the hunt but conducting a party of American tourists through the hills and revealing to them some of the more than four thousand paintings which had been discovered in addition to my original findings. We saw him again on the return from the hills and found him arguing and protesting to the tourist for not having paid him enough. Later we met him again with, outwardly, another perfect Bushman group of about twenty, all assembled in the great cave in the hills and offering hastily made bows and arrows and ostrich jewellery for sale to his clients.

Obviously the world and the archaeologists and anthro-

135

pologists, many just in search of a subject for another book or thesis for some master's degree, knew more about the hill than I ever did or could. The discovery of four thousand more paintings than the few I uncovered and the continuing digs around the base of the hills are a measure of how much more. But the hills had ceased to know them, and when Samutchao cried 'Gone! All gone with the spirits back into the earth where they came from', they could not know what we had experienced, and although their little memories could be more brightly lit than ever by their increase of knowledge, the source, the water, had returned for safe-keeping underground to the great memory. Not being known any longer, what they knew mattered less by the day, however great the monstrous bulk of knowledge grew.

I felt this with all the greater power and certainty because over the years, after reading every scrap of record I could find of what the vanished Bushman had told of himself to our forefathers, I had no doubt that these were the hills of their sacred First Spirit, the Dhxui referred to by Bleek and Lucy Lloyd, and the most ancient place of pilgrimage perhaps still identifiable in our country. Unlike the Lobatsi Hills, joined as they were to those supporting the escarpment of the great central plateau of Africa, they were on their own, an island of stone in an ocean of sand, and so, inevitably, an image of the ancient search of man for an identity and meaning of his own that will stand fast in the world of what the Buddhists call 'appearances' and 'a thousand floating things'. The peak of the highest hill, where, I was told by 'He who was left after the reaping', the greatest spirits were housed, was the Bushman's 'peak in Darien', and in spite of the psalmist I have quoted and Debenham's and my own powerful reaction, I cannot even guess at what welled up in the hunter's heart as he first caught sight, beyond the track of the animal he was hunting, of its blue staining the blue of heaven. The fact is that it aroused in the hunter so great an urge to create beyond himself that he covered the rocks with thousands of paintings. No National Gallery, Louvre, Hermitage or Prado can bear more convincing evidence to the significance of that unconquerable urge in man which makes him heed the great cry that goes out in *Upanishads*, 'O man, remember!', and turn back towards the memory which refuses to be forgotten.

I have recently been back to the hills again, just for a day, and the grip of the banalities of tourism has tightened. The little Bushman group was sadly diminished and struggling harder than ever for survival. The person who had led them so ably, they said, had been murdered, and only the bow-and-arrow maker of the little clan was there. He was still gentle as the unprovoked Bushman had always been, but now had an expression of ultimate resignation behind that glow in the dark mongolian eyes which I always thought was of the dawning of the first day of the first man on earth. The bows he was now making were purely perfunctory and, however plausible they may have looked in the parlour of some suburban home in the western world, would have been useless for the hunting which had once been both their livelihood and their passion. Indeed, the bow which I remembered from our first meeting was of different wood, stained dark with use but beautifully strung, and the arrows in his quiver so well dipped in poison that when I examined one closely he warned me, alarmed, not to bring the head any closer to my eyes. To demonstrate the danger he just tapped the arrow. Even so small a shock released a faint drift of poison dust from behind the arrow head which, he said, would have blinded me. The bows he now made were just for sale; but the one I first saw was a bow not only for enabling him to feed himself and his group but also an image of his urge to procreate and create beyond himself – the badge of the hunter on the spoor of meaning which leads to the self.

I went with him and the few friends with me on what I was certain would be my last walkabout in the hills. We retraced exactly my first walk and looked long at the paintings. It was heartening to note how untroubled and undimmed by time and weather they remained, where so much else around them had been eroded or erased. The imprint of the first painter's hand beneath the eland and giraffe on the honeyed sandstone overhang was like a hand stretched out in greeting, a hail and farewell across the abyss of time but one which, if clasped, in my own imagination, made the proffering and the clasping a now.

When we returned to the Bushman encampment, knowing so clearly that it was doomed and that my own effort to prevent the doom had utterly failed, the sadness I had felt with the passion of a child over Bushman history was rekindled and joined to outrage and humiliation that all I could give him now was some money, which could tranquillize but not cure some of the agony of the end he had to endure. As a reminder of how simple and clear his values were, how little he had asked of life and yet how much too much for us to give, there was a young woman in tears kneeling in the background. She was crying, soundless, with grief, feeling her honour impeached because, in pouring out some of their precious water from an ostrich-eggshell container, she had spilt a spoonful.

However, great as was the sense of the tragedy with which I left, I thought I would still be able to find some sort of comfort in the remote central desert. There I had some hope, bordering on a belief, that the desert, though deprived of its man, could still be intact in all other respects. As we were a very small group of just five, I had been

138

tempted to make straight for Paradise Pan, because I knew nothing now could give my friends a truer rendering of what the Kalahari was like when I first learnt to know it, but I had already had so many wounding lessons of the dangers of looking and going back over my tracks that I hesitated. I chose instead to camp at a place called Deception Pan, where some foretaste of that privileged world would inform us how wise it would be to press on, if at all, and kept the existence of Paradise Pan to myself.

It took only one night in Deception Pan to show me how impossible it was to go back to the reality I had known. I knew for certain now that the paradise we had recovered in the pan a generation before was lost. Even if it still held animals in the abundance and diversity which I had first encountered there, they would be animals who, like the world around this preparatory camp of ours, had lost their innocence and expelled man from their society as the wilderness around the pan was expelling him from its trust.

For instance, in all the years I had worked in the Kalahari I had never taken tents with me. I carried a light nylon tarpaulin which, in case of rain, I strung as a roof between my trucks and the trees. Otherwise we slept in the open every night, and although frequently we heard the lion roaring and other strange panting, snorting, snarling, hunting noises around us, followed very often by a leopard's cough, and occasionally the sound of a roving lone old elephant stripping the bark off a tree with a sound like gunshot, we trusted in our fire to keep a sufficient distance between them and us. But to my amazement, as we unloaded the trucks, which had been sent some days ahead of us to meet us at that point, we found that every one of us had been provided with a tent. Since the sky was clear and there was no prospect of rain whatsoever, I was just about to object to our camp organizer and tell him to put

139

the tents away when he told me that it could not be done. I asked why not, and he answered emphatically that it was not safe. He said that the lion and the leopard had lost their fear of fire, as they had long lost their fear of man by night, and that many people nowadays in the desert had been killed because they were not in some shelter or zipped up in a plastic tent. Only the night before our cook and other camp helpers had to stay locked in their trucks while they heard lion scavenging around the fire on which they had cooked their evening meal. When they got up in the morning, a plastic bucket of water left by the fire had disappeared, and it was only by following the spoor of a lioness that they found it abandoned nearly a mile away. Even our cook's indignation at such a lack of civility did not prevent me from rejoicing inwardly at the lioness's abhorrence of plastic, without losing my disillusionment over its effrontery. Animals in the desert had natural good manners when first I knew them.

However, had I been alone I believe I would have defied the warning, so much had I looked forward to sleeping again under the Kalahari sky, but it was not a risk I could take for my companions. As a result, one of the greatest gifts of the desert, a gift of sleep with nothing between oneself and the dark except a blanket, was denied to us until the very last night of all, when we pitched a special camp with a surround of trees and thorn to protect us and a fire of fires to stand like a sentry at Vesuvius between us and the night, and we slept in the open, the sky letting the starlight come down like dewdrops, and the lion keeping their distance and graciously serenading us from dusk to dawn. Those voices, and the shooting stars in between – two of the most stirring phenomena I know – went, plenipotentiary of the Kalahari I had known, straight to our hearts, and their echo, though receding down the canyon of the years in between, accompanied us all day over the skeleton-white flats of the great Makarikari stretched out as if it were that mythological plain of which the Africans spoke in my childhood, so vast and so empty when crossing it that the heart within cried out 'Oh mother, I am lost!' How lost, indeed, for I remembered the Makarikari when it retained enough water at one end to be aflame with flamingo fire at dawn.

Not only had the lion changed but the milder antelopes, the gentlest gazelles, even the little steenbuck with his concentration of purity shining like a lamp in the great pupils of his wide eyes, who would always find time to stand and stare, now on our first approach got up in alarm, and ran without looking back. The gemsbok would not pause in his shade under an umbrella of thorn to look and see who we were but was on his feet and instantly running. All in all, the change in the mood of animals and birds expressed a degree of the alienation of man even greater and more alarming than the total suppression of stone-age culture and rejection of the Bushman. I thought of the bitter truth in a remark made by an old white hunter in another story of mine: 'Should the last man vanish from the earth tomorrow, there is not a plant, bird or animal who would not breathe a sigh of relief.' I might have felt, perhaps, that I could improve on it by including in the relief also that of our mother earth, had not this desert – through its suffering, forebearance, patience and lack of vanity – given such clear proof of bearing all, of which, according to St Paul in the New Testament, only *charitas* – love beyond itself – is capable, and which, despite all, she maintains at heart, still and forever more.

All the way out of the desert I kept thinking back many years to the moment when I realized that it would be fatal to expose the desert to human husbandry, and that its great

141

contribution to life could be in its preservation as an area stretching from the foothills of the Transvaal, the borders of the Shashi, Limpopo and Zambezi down to the Molopo river, up and across the border of South West Africa to the Namib Hills, north to Mossamedes, taking the Okavango firmly in its sweep, and all the rest where a rich sandveld, turned fertile by millions of years of natural rehabilitation, could be turned into a last keep of the original life of Africa, a keep unlike any other, because it would be enriched as a fortress also of our aboriginal man. The desert, even its Okavango delta, clearly had no contribution that was at all lasting to make to the market economics of our exacting technological day, but it could have a great, spiritually enriching future as a place where man could have access, as it were, to creation's original bureau of standards and from time to time come to measure the values of his being against the master values as they were in the beginning.

Some of us had indeed already started to work for some such dream when the events which now divide Africa so tragically against itself overtook us and, for the moment, as far as the physical world is concerned, the light that was in the dream lies like a lamp shattered in the dust. The hope that remains is the kind of Promethean hope which has to create from its own wreck the thing that it contemplates, and it is a hope that is singularly in the keeping of the great memory with which we began.

On this occasion of disillusionment and apocalyptic revelation of which I speak, the night before I started out on this little journey I spoke to a distinguished geologist who had worked for many years in the Kalahari and who had even, briefly, known my mother when she herself had been drawn to the Kalahari and found water where people said no water could ever be found, and had established herself at the very Stilton where my own physical experience of the desert began. I asked this geologist in what sort of timescale people like myself who love the Kalahari had to think of it. From what the rocks, the sands and all those deep and dry watercourses told him, he said, it could not be less than one thousand million years, which I am certain is barely a step in the march of creation. So, somewhere, waiting to be unlocked in that memory, I am certain, is a pattern of life that will transcend and transfigure this arid and desperate moment of time wherein we live, and the first move towards that unlocking, I believe, is to absorb the horror of the story of what we have all done to the first man of Africa and the horror of what we are doing now to the plants and the animals that for one thousand million years at least were safe and multiplying in his and the desert's keeping. Never has it been so important and urgent, if human life on earth is not to fail the purpose which created it and gives it meaning, to begin again its ancient quest of seeking to remember what remembers us. It is because of my own brief experience of the power and the glory of this memory made manifest in the desert that I am certain, in its own time and after its own fashion, it will not allow us to fail, even if that means inflicting on us, as it has so often had to do in the past, the disaster we need to heed.

The Great Memory

'Et venio in campos et lata praetoria memoriae'
ST AUGUSTINE
'And so I come to the fields and wide mansions
of memory'

I HAVE TOLD the story of the Bushman of southern Africa in books and films and talks to people in many parts of the world. I should have done more and done it better; but I have the melancholy justification that I did all I could do in my time and place. The Chinese have an ancient saying that the wise man speaks but once. I cannot claim the wisdom that this saying presupposes; but I have a feeling that it applies even to the not-so-wise, and perhaps most of all to the foolish. I have no temptation, therefore, to go back on my tracks. Unfinished as the history remains, its completion is best left to those whose business is history, and who have the relevant dedication, the love of the subject and the training, possessed for instance by Jane Taylor, author of *Testament to the Bushmen*. All that I can and should still do, perhaps, is to add to this tragic story of the Bushmen more of my experience of his being, and the role he has played in my imagination, so that the horror of his elimination over the gruesome millennia behind us can be fully understood. I do not intend to write about it as a piece of historicity but as a profoundly significant event which points unerringly to a cruel imperviousness in our so-called civilization.

One of the most deceptive of popular half-truths is the saying that history repeats itself. Only unredeemed, unrecognized, misunderstood history, I believe, repeats itself, and remains a dark, negative and dangerous dominant on the scene of human affairs. Although the Bushman has gone, what he personified, the patterns of spirit made flesh and blood in him and all he evoked or provoked in us, lives on as a ghost within ourselves. This is no subjective illusion of mine evoked by the special relationship I have always had with him. Something like him, a first man, is dynamic in the underworld of the spirit of all men, no matter of what race, creed or culture. I know this as an empiric fact because of all the books I have written and films I have made about the Bushman; his story has been translated into all languages except Chinese, travelled the world and been taken into the hearts of millions as if it were food in a universal famine of spirit. What this means for our own time depends in the first instance on our redis-covery of these patterns in ourselves and our readiness to cease being accessories after the fact of diminished con-sciousness, of which murder is the ultimate symbol. As Hamlet in his haunted fortress had it, when the time is out of joint, as ours certainly is, the readiness is all.

It has seemed increasingly urgent to me, therefore, to look into the causes of this imperviousness and reinterpret the Bushman's story in the light of my own day. Not only the present but the future depends on a constant reinterpre-tation of history and a re-examination of the state and nature of human consciousness. Both these processes are profoundly and mysteriously interdependent and doomed to failure without a continuous search after self-knowledge, since we and our awareness are inevitably the main instru-ments of the interpretation.

This for me is not as simple as it may sound. The obstacles encountered by all who try to serve the Word, whole as it was in the beginning, are always formidable but never more so than when they seek to throw light on areas of our aboriginal darkness where consciousness has left an infinity of meaning, unchosen and untransfigured like

148

ghosts of the unborn in a night without moon, stars or end. Once launched on this voyage of exploration, it is significant how much easier it is to confine oneself to studying the external and visible reality, the mechanistics of archaic communities and the behaviour of man. There is a great deal of self-satisfaction and an almost tangible sense of achievement to be found in a demonstrable approach to life. I imagine this has a great deal to do with the absorption of anthropologists in the outward pattern of 'primitive' societies and their dutiful recording of aboriginal behaviour and ritual. This recording can hardly be done without condescension, and it is diminishing to both observer and observed when the latter is almost exclusively regarded as an object of study and the theme of yet another PhD thesis.

The real trouble began for me, as it has done for countless others, when I sought to understand imaginatively the primitive in ourselves, and in this search the Bushman has always been for me a kind of frontier guide. Imagination shifts and passes, as it were, through a strange customs post on the fateful frontier between being and unrealized self, between what is and what is to come. The questions that have to be answered before the imagination is allowed through are not new but have to be redefined because of their long neglect and the need for answers to be provided in the idiom of our own day. For instance, in what does man now find his greatest meaning? Indeed, what is meaning itself for him and where its source? What are the incentives and motivations of his life when they clearly have nothing to do with his struggle for physical survival? What is it in him that compels him, against all reason and all the prescriptions of law, order and morality, still to do repeatedly what he does not consciously want to do? What is this dark need in the life of the individual and society for tragedy and disaster? Since the two world wars that have occurred

149

in my own lifetime, disorder and violence have become increasingly common on the world scene. Surely these things are rooted in some undiscovered breach of cosmic law or they would be eminently resistible and would not be allowed to occur? Where indeed does one propose to find an explanation for the long history of human failure? How can one hope to understand this aspect of man and his societies, and comprehend a scene littered with ruins and piled high with dunes of time which mark the places where countless cultures have vanished because men would not look honestly, wholly and steadily into the face of their inadequacies? The answers to none of these questions are available unless one is prepared through profound self-knowledge to re-learn the grammar of a forgotten language of self-betrayal, and in so doing the meaning of tragedy and disaster. It is the ineluctable preliminary to our emancipation, especially for those priests and artists who have been subverting themselves and the societies which they are dedicated to preserve. Unless one is honestly prepared to do so, one is warned at this crepuscular immigration post that one had better not cross the frontier.

For the English-speaking world the most significant example of such an imagination shift is to be found, of course, in Shakespeare's *Hamlet*. It was preceded by works in which Shakespeare celebrates the beauty, the potentials for happiness, the plausible attractions and surface patterns of the outer world. But suddenly it is as if the wind of time from some absolute frontier of the universe brings him a scent of the existence of a denied meaning that is far more than surface beauty, and so much greater than either the happiness or unhappiness encountered on the worldly scene. And at once it is as if, with Hamlet, man crosses, not only for himself but for all men, this long-shunned frontier of the spirit, and from there begins years of journeying of a new kind. The journey this time inevitably goes down into an underworld of mind and time, where man is confronted not only with all the inadequacies and consequences of his wordly consciousness but also faces, alone and unsupported by a familiar pattern of living, the stark necessity of making his own choice between good and evil, truth and untruth, before he is free to move on towards the wholeness that their opposition so paradoxically serves. Shakespeare, I believe, becomes, in his great phrase, one of 'God's spies' and takes on himself 'the mystery of things' so *utterly* (as the Bushmen would have it) that he could come to rest in the conclusion: 'Men are such stuff as dreams are made on'. But even as dream material Shakespeare in *The Tempest* is still faced with an ending that would be despair, 'unless I be relieved by prayer'. Why prayer? Because it is the symbol both of man's recognition of the existence of, and his dependence on, a power of creation beyond his conscious understanding, and greater than life and time, that time which Einstein described not as a condition in which life exists so much as a state of mind. In prayer, there is an image of certain promise that through this recognition and this remembrance and surrender of the part to a sense of the whole, Shakespeare could summon help from the heart of the universe to live the final portion of the overall dream with which his art was invested and to which his flesh and blood was entrusted.

All this may seem as remote from the Bushmen and stone-age culture as to be irrelevant. Yet in reality it has an *a priori* significance not only for understanding the nature of primitive being but for preventing the contraction of individual consciousness, which is such an alarming symptom of our collectivist day, and promoting the enlargement of individual consciousness into an expanding awareness on which the renewal of our societies depends. The collec-

151

tivist and intellectual turned 'intellectualist', the promoter of 'isms' of the intellect that are to the sanity of being and spirit what viruses are to the body, will no doubt find it absurd, but it is precisely because the Bushman has been a scout and frontier guide to me from infancy in the same dark labyrinthine underworld of human nature which Shakespeare entered precipitately with *Hamlet*, that I have been compelled to tell the world about him. From time to time during my life I try to reappraise what the Bushman has done for me and here I do so probably for the last time. I cannot disguise that for many years I lost conscious sight of him as I went my own wilful way, but instinctively he was always there and bound never to mislead or fail. He could not fail, as I realized looking back on to the vortex of the movement which he started in my imagination, because I recognized with the clarity and precision of instinct of a child that he was still charged with magic and wonder. He was an example of a 'spy of God', to follow beyond the well-dug trenches of the aggressive Calvinist consciousness of our community into some no-man's land of the spirit where he had taken upon him the mystery of things. He, too, was from the beginning 'such stuff as dreams are made on' and had soldiered on in the field where the prophetic soul of the wide world also dreamed of things to come.

The essence of this is self-evident, I believe, and confirmed by the elements in the matter which first forced their way into my conscious imagination. I do not know how old I was when the first grit of external fact was placed in position and the pearl within began to form. All I know is that it was before the age of five when I first began to read by myself with an acceleration and absorption which surprised as well as somewhat alarmed the extravert pioneering world into which I was born. It came in a way I still find significant, very soon after the visitation of the great comet in our star-sown sky, with months of earthquakes and great tremors of rock and ground and a terrible drought which still presides in my recollection as the greatest fear my being has ever encountered. Though the exact time cannot be determined, the moment itself is definite and clear.

I was being read to by my mother in the evening of one of the rare occasions she was at home. My father was still alive and a lawyer much in demand. As a politician and statesman he was away a great deal and she never failed to accompany him, because, great and natural mother as she was, she knew that for all the assurance and authority with which he moved in the world, there was a neglected child in him that needed mothering, even more than her own children did. But when at home she gave us unendingly and impartially of herself with an unfailing abundance that still seems miraculous to me. One of her most precious ways of giving was through her love of stories and her gift of telling them with the capacity of total recall cultivated in her by the Hottentot and Bushman fragments of humanity who found asylum in my grandfather's home – 'Bushman's Spring'. She read superbly – so much so that the reading of the first of several books by Dickens, *Nicholas Nickleby*, lives on so clearly in my mind that I have never been tempted to re-read the book or see vamped-up versions of it on stage and television because my memory holds an experience that cannot be bettered and in a sense is sacred. But on this first occasion she was reading a story particu-larly chosen for me because she knew that I shared her own love of the aboriginal people of Africa and their stories in a way that none of her other children did. She knew especially that through the presence and influence of my first Bushman nurse, who went under the European name 'Klara' because her own was too difficult for ordinary pioneering tongues, my imagination was involved as much with the world of the Bushman as of the European.

It is worth pausing to note how early the coincidences came to crowd in on the imagination of the child that I was, perhaps as the signs of confirmation that the classical age of China held them to be. They came as unsolicited messengers bearing the wonder so necessary for the enlargement of the human spirit, and a sense of a reality too strange, as T. S. Eliot had it, for misunderstanding. First of all, there was 'Bushman's Spring'. It was built in the heart of great Bushman earth and within sight of what was once a precious source of unfailing Bushman water. On the hills beyond the spring there were the circles of stone walls raised by that great branch of stone-age civilization, the Bushmen of the plains, to protect them against the frost and thin winds of ice from the Basuto Mountains of the Night. The stone shelters were unroofed because rain was never abundant or regular, and was always welcome. My grandfather who had built 'Bushman's Spring' had frequently fought against the Bushman. He had helped to organize the raid that eliminated the last of the Bushmen in the southern Free State, except for two little boys, whom he took back to his home and who, as little old men, were to be my companions when I was a child. Above all, there was my Bushman nurse, Klara. She said her name meant 'light', and, for me, she was bathed in wonder: the light of rainbow morning, a crystal day and magic lantern evening, playing on the bright blue beads of glass of a heavy necklace around the smooth apricot skin of her throat. I remember her face as one of the most beautiful I have ever known; oval, with a slightly pointed chin, high cheek bones, wide, large and rather slanted eyes full of a dark, glowing light as of the amber of the first glow on earth shining through the brown of evening on man's first day. These features gave her an oddly Chinese appearance especially as I never saw the thick, short, matted hair which was always wrapped in cottons of the brightest colours. No one ever shone more brightly in my emotions. She remained at the deep centre of the love of the feminine which has given me so much. Not even my mother meant so much to me although I loved and admired my mother so that all she gave me can be measured only by imponderables. Although she died many years ago, not a day goes by without its outstanding events compelling the thought, 'I must write and tell mother about it.'

As a result, this still, high-veld evening when Klara had put me to bed and held my hand while she listened as intently as I to my mother's reading, is near and alive, in spite of the decades that separate me from it. This shrill, brittle, self-important life of today is by comparison a grave-yard where the living are dead and the dead are alive and talking in the still, small, clear voice of a love and trust in life that we have for the moment lost. She was reading to me the Wilhelm Bleek and Lucy Lloyd account of one of the greatest Bushman stories, 'The Lynx, the Hyena and the Morning Star'. This story had appeared in some learned journal in the Cape and I think it is so much a key Bushman story that I have retold it and assayed some of the riches it holds for me in *The Heart of the Hunter*. No detailed retelling of it is therefore necessary now. All I need as a frame for the portrait of the occasion is to define its theme as one of primordial jealousy. It is a story of the irresistible envy the ignoble are compelled always to have for the noble, the deprived for the enriched, the evil for the good and all that results from what my French grandmother called *nostalgie de la boue*. As such it is an orchestration in its own primitive counterpoint of the same pattern which sees

Iago undo all that is brave in Othello and extinguish the beauty and innocence that is Desdemona.

The shape of the story is from beginning to end pure and true. It is of a perfect proportion of beauty that is for me always as alarming as it is enchanting. The Morning Star, the 'Foot of the Day' as Klara also called it, has chosen a female lynx as a bride. It was still the time before the coming of Mantis and his fire that frightened all natural things away and left man for the first time alone in the dark by his glowing coal. All on earth and in the universe were still members and family of the early race seeking comfort and warmth through the long, cold night before the dawning of individual consciousness in a togetherness which still gnaws like an unappeasable homesickness at the base of the human heart. No match of the masculine and feminine could have been more precise, or have a greater potential of harmony. Just as the Morning Star was the brightest and greatest hunter among the hunting stars of that hemisphere, the lynx, for the Bushman as for me, was the most star-like of animals on earth. The temptations for the Morning Star to make the wrong choice in the animal kingdom of Africa must have been almost overwhelming. There has never been another such kingdom to equal it in the numbers, wealth, variety, power, glory, beauty, tenderness and forcefulness of its natural subjects. Among the aristocratic cat families of Africa alone competition for the Morning Star's hand must have been formidable, and one considers the claims of the cats first because they walked alone in the forests of the night of Africa as the Morning Star hunted alone in the great plain of heaven on the rim between night and day. In such a position, with his experience of the power of the night and privileged vision into the heart of the light, the Morning Star caught the imagination of the first people of Africa in the meaningful and precise way which all the

156

world's star-conscious mythologies have had a knack of doing.

Such an exalted element of heaven inevitably demanded to be joined to an equal and opposite life on earth. Only a cat who walked alone could be suitable for so fateful a joining of the most illuminated masculine transfiguration in heaven to the love of creation instinctive in the feminine earth. The claims of the lion in this regard must have been most powerful, plausible and eloquent because it too was a cat that went a way of its own and tended to be individual and specific among the crowds and herds of natural life in Africa. Moreover the lion combined such a formidable complex of talents, spirit and energies that he was universally accepted as the king of beasts of Africa and no feminine being could have ever been more fierce, urgent and triumphant in the cause of procreation of the natural life in Africa than the lioness.

But somehow such a marriage would have been disproportionate. The lion was too big, too physical, proud, domineering and self-sufficient and would have unbalanced any close relationship with so sensitive and finely poised a being as the Morning Star. The leopard, too, had its own matchless qualities but again there were basic disproportions of size and hubris of appetite and aggression to make it unsuitable, not least of all in the matter of its spots. Who could imagine, as Klara explained after my mother's reading, making us laugh with relief at the clarity and authority of her interpretation, the Morning Star – unstained and clearcut as the diamond in my mother's ring presented to my father by de Beers on their engagement – going about with a fudged and spotty bride? No, it could only be the lynx.

I remember how this conclusion quickened my pulse and warmed me through because, young as I was, I had seen the lynx already and knew him well. We had a couple breeding happily as pets on our farm but what was more, in a remote complex of the hills which cut across the centre of it, one of which was high enough to earn it the title of mountain, several families still lived unthreatened in their natural state. I had been taken many times by senior members of a family of nature worshippers just to observe them. There was one favourite place where trellises and lattices of shade plaited in thick screens of bright green broom and blue brushes, dark wild olives and touch-me-not shrubs were presided over by some giant euphorbia, like candelabra in a Byzantine church. The intense shadow thrown by an immense overhang of rock going grey with time rippled like a wind on the water of a deep pond. There, repeatedly, I had seen how bright with flame and quick with light and colour the lynx was, so that his movement in that dark surround was like the flicker and flame of a vestal lamp. It explained why no pioneer ever spoke of him by any other name than red-cat.

But no sooner had the fateful logic and harmony of the union of Morning Star and lynx been established than all was darkened by the intrusion of the shadow of shadows. The female hyena appeared out of the night that was native to the carrion of which it was the dark, dishonoured royalty and without pretence or shame walked into the scene, naked with jealousy of the lynx. The turmoil and heightening of drama implicit in this shadowy entry were immediate.

I knew the hyena as well as the Morning Star and the lynx. The mountain of which I have spoken was not for nothing called the Mountain of the Wolves. The wolf was the pioneering name for the large, striped, powerfully shouldered hyena which could deprive a cow of its udder with one snap of its jaws. Our mountain was full of them. I had come to know the hyena so well already that in the half-light of an early morning on a long journey by carriage and horse with my mother, I had looked one in the eyes from some two yards away as it stood among the bushes beside the road where we had stopped to give our horses a breather. Its eyes, made for the dark, were already blurred, and it held its head still so that it could examine with its nose the air between us. That look was one of my most unnerving experiences. It was especially frightening because of a profound melancholy in the hyena's eye, beyond reason and resolution, deepened with a knowledge that it could never walk openly as do all other animals in a world of light. It was frightening, too, because it revealed a terrible insecurity, a suspicion and sense of irrevocable exile unrelieved by any hint of trust in life. It could trust nothing except its unsleeping cunning and deviousness and there was thus no discernible centre of integrity around which it could weave, like other animals, a permanent pattern of vivid being and doing. Indeed, it was so utterly aboriginal that it was like chaos and old night made flesh and blood, and forced me to turn away and hide my face in my mother's lap, full of a fear which had no name. Many years later I was to encounter a summing up of the experience in a Bushman expression, 'the time of the hyena', used the day I heard it to describe a state of madness which unbearable tragedy had imposed upon a young Bushman woman; and again still later for describing moments when not only the light of the mind was invaded by darkness, but life itself was overcast with the approach of the goodnight of death. To add to my heightening apprehension, I recognized the dread power of jealousy.

However much the grown-up world might pretend to be immune to such primordial urges, we children knew better. However angelic the best of us may have looked, we were not in danger of thinking of ourselves as 'only babies small,

159

dropped from the sky'. This embarrassing euphemism featured in a song popular among 'respectable' young women of the day who had been shamed into using it by Calvinist indoctrination. Exposed to all the processes of birth, procreation and death that went on around us in the natural world from the moment we ourselves were born, we had a more realistic view of life. We, therefore, instantly recognized, feared and were perpetually perplexed by adult hypocrisy and prejudices in primordial things. We knew and both gloried and suffered daily from the fact that we were as open and subject to storm from all the primeval urges as the sea is to the great winds that travel the world and time. How could I, for instance, as one of fifteen children, not begin with jealousy of the child that displaced me? Had it not been that the love available in our own vast family was impartially accessible and at the service of all, envy, jealousy and competitiveness could have distorted us. But happily I could not recollect a single act of parental favouritism. Scrutinizing the family record as I have over many years, I am uplifted by it. It was not until my mother was dying that I discovered that she had had a favourite after all without ever having succumbed to favouritism.

One began to learn early, therefore, that this basic form of insecurity, jealousy, could not be experienced without damage to oneself and others, and ultimately one can only be redeemed from it and the fears it engenders, by a kind of emotion of self-courage. This has to be induced by reconciliation with the valid needs of others living in an atmosphere of love. This selfless love was the centre of our family. It remains an irrefutable social and individual premise, that no culture has ever been able to provide a better shipyard for building stormproof vessels for the journey of man from the cradle to the grave than the individual nourished in a loving family. This, though, is still a mere

160

abbreviation, but what I have said is perhaps enough to indicate the impact that the appearance of the hyena made on me and explain the gallop of fear that took over as it proclaimed its intention of breaking up the marriage of the Morning Star and taking the place of the lynx.

The way the hyena set about it was sheer black magic and so convincing that I had no need then for a conscious grasp of the universal symbolism of what was happening and of which I attempted a cursory exegesis in *The Heart of the Hunter*. By the power of her dark art, she transformed the food of the lynx into a poison that progressively deprived the lynx of her will and spirit to live. Each stage of the deterioration was illuminated in the story with a bright bead of detail, as in those necklaces the primitive world of Africa prepared in mourning for their dead, until the final and seemingly unavoidable eclipse of the lynx and her banishment into outer darkness were imminent, and my heart was almost black with dread. Then, suddenly, the hope which was almost at an end in me stirred again.

The world of fairy-tale and folklore proclaims with irrefutable accuracy that no matter how many evil feminine forces and wicked masculine ones in the shapes of ugly sisters, witches, giants, uncles, step-fathers and step-mothers combine against creation on earth, somewhere always there is something built into life to counter them: a small, often despised something, a mere Tom Thumb, a crumpled old man, a humble, simple peasant couple like Baucis and Philemon, or even just a being of potential nobility disguised as a repulsive toad. In the story of the lynx the good fairy appeared in the shape of the lynx's vigilant sister who acted immediately and decisively. Just as the apparently doomed lynx was cast out of her hut and the hyena moved in, the gallant sister went to warn the Morning Star and told him plainly that his light on earth, his love of the lynx, and the reality of his own feminine soul, was about to be extinguished. Just as the love that is feminine cannot endure without male amour, and male power has no meaning without a feminine soul to serve, so the Morning Star instantly recognized the universal implication of the hyena's threat to heaven and earth, and took instant action. Fitting an arrow to his bow, and spear in hand, the story describes in language worthy of Blake's 'tiger bright', how the Morning Star descends swiftly to the earth, his eyes full of the fire of a just anger. The violence of his approach sends the hyena rushing from the hut in great panic. Swerving to avoid the spear of the Morning Star, its hind leg catches on the coals of the fire which were burning as usual on the scooped-out place in front of the hut. The hyena was burned so badly that it was condemned to the lopsided walk that it still has to this day. From that moment the lynx recovered, was fully restored in her honour and affections, and she and all manner of things were well.

I could not have been more relieved and happy by such an ending and embraced both my mother and Klara in tears of sheer joy. I was all the happier on being assured that the reason why the Morning Star continues to sit with an eye so bright between night and day is that he has learned the lesson that not only are the forces of darkness and evil which the hyena personifies on earth built into the foundations of the universe and indestructible, but also that it is only by an exercise of everlasting vigilance on the frontiers of the mind that he can defeat them and prevent a triumph of night over day.

The effect on me of this story was so great that I woke early in the dark next morning, and slipped out of the karosses, the rugs of soft animal skins in which I always slept in good weather outside on the wide verandah which

162

surrounded our home. For a moment I hesitated. The howl of the perpetual recurring Ishmael element in life which is implicit in the voice of the hyena reached me and seemed to change into a minor scale the major key of the music of the stars which resounded over the vast full-leafed garden beyond. There stood the trees in their long robes of leaves, priests of their natural kingdom, heads bowed as if calling for prayer from the minaret of the world. For a moment I shivered with an involuntary spasm of the fear that the hyena's role in the story had induced in me the night before, but then I recalled the impulse which had delivered me from sleep. I went slowly to the very edge of the raised verandah and looked over and out to the east of the immense garden, and there, just lifting itself clear over the dark crown of fig trees by the wall around the orchard, was the Morning Star. Perhaps as a result of the story, it appeared to me brighter than ever, its eye fiercer. An arrow was fitted to its bow, a spear was in its hand, and the tips of arrow and spear were aimed at the area of darkness on earth where the hyena had just given a howl of self-pity, complaint, carrion intent and shame for itself. The rush of emotion was so great that it stays with me still. It provided the nursery in which a great tree of conviction and abiding hope grew, and I was confirmed in the knowledge that there is a vigilant and indestructible element of light in life that transcends night and day on earth as in heaven.

As for the hyena, the villain of the piece, a strange regret in me because it was not killed was slowly resolved. Over the years the hyena has taken its proper position in my mind. I realized why it had to live and have a hind leg permanently marked by fire. Fire was to become the great image of consciousness for me, and that seal of fire on the hyena was an assurance that the evil it represents has been clearly marked. It is a sign of our conscious knowledge and experience of the living reality and power of evil. For all its dominion in the night of our unawareness and lack of vigilance, evil is so marked that man is free at last to choose between light and dark, good and evil; a freedom not of escape or evasion but a heightening of man's obligations to creation.

All this and much more was in the seed sown in me by a Bushman story heard at a very early age. It is the most striking and unanswerable evidence of man's need for enrolment in a true story if he is to endure and live his way towards his life's answer. The very next day, by a process of restless questioning from me and solicitous answers from Klara and my mother, I learned how Wilhelm Bleek and Lucy Lloyd had collected many stories such as this.

They drew them out of a group of little Bushmen convicts, condemned to the hardest labour: work on a new breakwater in Cape Town harbour. The crime had only been one of killing, when hungry, a sheep from one of the large flocks owned by men, white and black, who had stolen all their land from them. One of the most prolific sources of stories was a little Bushman called Xhabbo – a name meaning Dream, which Klara hastened to explain was a not uncommon Bushman name, because what could be more manly and responsible than to be connected to a dream. In due course I was given a copy of a colour portrait of Xhabbo of the Dream. It is still with me, together with a snapshot of a Bushman taken in the heart of the Kalahari some thirty-five years after Xhabbo first came into my reckoning. I keep the Kalahari photograph because it is of the hunter who told me one day when, greedy for more stories, I had exhausted him with questions. 'You see it is very difficult because there is a dream dreaming us.' And what could be closer to Shakespeare's prophetic soul, dreaming of things to come?

164

From that moment of illumination from the light of a star story, my appetite for Bushman stories, myth and legend grew and I clamoured for more. For years Klara and my mother complied. And as my interest in Bushman stories grew, the attractions of the fairy-tales of the Western world which were also thrust on me lessened, only the Greek myths and stories from the Old Testament still holding my imagination. It was not that I despised the Brothers Grimm, Hans Christian Andersen or Andrew Lang, but their characters were comparatively pale and remote proxies of those of men, animals and plants that were the heroic and anti-heroic material and settings of the Bushman stories. These were peopled with an immense cast of characters from the physical world into which I had been born and were the essential stuff of my imagination, dreams and being. There were even times when I felt sorry for European children fed on such anaemic food, so deprived of the trace-elements and forms of natural life that were lightning conductors of miracle and magic in my childhood. The more complex stories and literature of the West only moved into my imagination when the last Bushman story had been told.

Even then I seemed to know that the written literature which dominated my education and imagination was a mere dwarf poised on the shoulders of a giant of unwritten and oral literature that preceded it. It could never have had the meaning it possesses for me were it not for the stories of the living word which the Bushman had so reverently prepared for me. These stories, populated by the vivid natural life I understood and loved, remain with me. What I love most about them is that they are never obvious, and are intuitively Shakespearian in their wisdom. The Bushmen are never taken in by mere appearances and surface attractions. For instance, they are immune to the blasphemies of size, numbers and giant power, and they do not measure the significance of man or beast by the ability to overcome and destroy those weaker than themselves. The heroes of the Bushmen, indeed, were almost invariably drawn from the physically insignificant.

The stone-age civilization, of which I heard echoes in the Bushman stories of my childhood, spread over the greater part of southern Africa. It existed wherever the Bushman had enough permanent water and sufficient rain to make the earth fruitful. In Africa, nutritious roots, bulbs, tubers, wild fruit, nuts and berries grew in abundance. In no other continent was there so much game to be had. Consequently, the Bushman's struggle for survival was never so desperate as to engage the whole of his days. He had the leisure even to gather and add to his food an archaic honey that was like light on darkness and brought sweetness to the many rough and bitter tastes endured by his spartan palate. Typically he raised the search for honey into a kind of sacramental adventure. He joined to him as allies, not only the bird known as the honey-guide, one of the most miraculous elements of the air, a prototype of Ariel almost, but also the ratel or honey-badger, a Calibanesque phenomenon so close to the earth and its plants as to be almost clay made flesh. There was a magic and religious revelation in this alliance, and to see it in successful action, as I have been privileged to do, is to be overawed by a sense of how near the first men were to the miraculous. From the beginning, the human being was devoutly involved with nature.

Perhaps uniquely, therefore, the stone-age Bushman had leisure, and this explains why and how he could evolve the richest and most complex form of stone-age civilization in Africa. That is why in *The Heart of the Hunter* I turned to the record of Bushman civilization and gave it preference over others I knew as well. I use the word 'civilization' rather than culture deliberately because of the Bushman's

166

extraordinary achievement in the detail of his daily routine, and in the realm of the spirit through his myths, legends, stories, music, dancing and paintings. They are all without trace of the hubris to which Greek, Roman and Hebraic man were so prone that they feared it as the greatest source of evil. The inspiration of Bushman painting embraced not only 'magical' aspirations but all aspects of man and his surroundings, from the immediacies of his day to the most complex and subtle intimations of reality and immortality. Specialists in this field are usually not artists themselves. They tend to approach their subject with the preconceived attitudes imposed on them by the basic assumptions of their own discipline, conceived in a cultural context that could not be more remote and alien to that of the Bushman. I know of none among those who have written on Bushman art, for instance, who has thought it necessary to acquire in depth a knowledge of symbolism, comparative myth-ology and psychology. They need to recognize that the dream is the gateway to the meaning of our prehistoric past on which our sense of continuity and the totality of history depends. Indeed history is nothing if it is not so illuminated. Life is made intuitive and instinctive and inscribed in the forgotten language of the dream and its symbols. Dreams finally are the main instruments with which the meaning and achievement of stone-age culture can be decoded, and the quintessential humanity of the Bushman unlocked. Indeed the Bushman was and, to an extent, remains what we, increasingly cut off from our natural selves and the little that is left of the natural world, can only dream of today. It is a constant source of amazement and of hope to me that I have not been to a continent or island, from East to West, where I have not found that when men fall asleep something like the Bushman awakes and beckons them.

Happily my introduction to the larger stone-age man

came at a time when he had not altogether vanished. I had only to ask and stretch out my hand to hear his authentic voice and touch his warm, smooth, apricot skin, and be startled by the electricity of immediate, utter humanity with which it sparked and against which we, in an arrogance of mind and hubris of our technological mastery of nature, are insulated. An illustration of this impoverished approach to stone-age man, for instance, can be found in the work of a most worthy scholar who has dedicated his life to a study of Bushman painting and yet describes perhaps the greatest and certainly most tragic story ever told by the Bushman, as one of the funniest he has ever read. I feel certain this is because his studies were conducted in ignorance of the symbolism, mythology and, above all, the cypher of dreams in which their meaning is encoded.

It was not surprising that, as my fund of stories grew, there were moments when the line so arbitrarily drawn by the exactions of contemporary consciousness between waking and dreaming seemed to vanish. I would often feel as if I were on an enchanted island in the sea of time at the still centre of the terrible storms, the aftermath of war, unrest, loss of faith and the prelude to a catastrophic sequel which dominated the world of my parents. On this island I was surrounded with strange music and, through these stories, it was as if the clouds for me too had opened as they had done even on Shakespeare's Caliban and allowed unimagined riches and splendours to pour over me, so that I wondered whether I was really awake and longed to sleep and dream again.

These stories were increasingly dominated by the Praying Mantis, the Hottentots' god as my ancestors called him when they landed at the Cape of Good Hope three hundred years ago. They attributed him to the pastoral Hottentots, an ancient nomadic people of Africa who were closest to the Bushman. Had they paused to ask the Bushman and tried to throw the tenuous bridge of a desire for comprehension across the abyss of spirit and being which divided them from him, they would have known that the Mantis was a Bushman and not a Hottentot god.

The Hottentots had their own highly evolved image of a god, subtle, complex, most evocative and, for me, intensely moving and real. They called him Heitse-Eibib and saw him in the red of the dawn which they held to be the blood of the wounds he had incurred in his everlasting battle with night for day. I was surrounded in childhood by even more Hottentot than Bushman survivors because the place where I was born was once the capital of what we as children thought of as the kingdom of the Griquas, one of the last coherent Hottentot clans driven into the interior by the white tide of immigration from the Cape to the north. In the process they were subjected by well-meaning missionaries to a strange injection of biblical myths and stories which did not eliminate Heitse-Eibib but merely drove him intact to the core and inner keep of their spirit. They not only showered stories about him on me but at moments of crisis and emphasis still swore in his name. He became so real to me that I found poetic justice and continuity in the fact that he should follow in the spoor of the Morning Star, an heroic and wounded protagonist of light in the van of the passing-out parade of the military academy of the sky. The Griquas had taught me that his spirit was also always in the wind, and I learned to feel his presence stirring the leaves of the wild olives and great broom bushes where I crouched with burning cheeks and smarting, bare feet for relief from the heat of the great flaming days of summer. But he would be most near me when I contemplated one of the heaps of smooth pebbles piled high in his honour in places from what is Zululand in the southeast today to where the mythological sun went down in the far west over deep ancient river-beds that run no more and where his people are no longer known. These piles were raised by Hottentots bound, out of their constant awareness of what was due to their sense of creation, to deposit pebbles in recognition of Heitse-Eibib's all-pervasive presence and help, wherever they had forded a river or stream. In my childhood those pebbles were as much wayside shrines to me as those encountered by knights of the Round Table and Holy Grail on their quest.

Knowing the stories they had evoked in the Hottentot imagination, the piles of pebbles were more sacred to me than the Calvinist churches I was marched into like a young recruit by the implacable sergeant-majors of law-bound elders thrice on Sundays. They produced a sense of the mystery of creation far more intense than anything in the Bible, many as were the stories in that Book that I loved. Many Bible stories in any case did not contradict or make implausible either Mantis or Heitse-Eibib, but placed them as neighbours in the inner propinquity of the authentic dimension of religious experience. In this regard, it could be said that by the time I reached the ripe old age of five, I was either as confused or enlightened and enriched by this exciting input of stories from these aboriginal sources as any Hottentot. More consciously and most important, I found them a great bridge from the primordial world of the child into the here and now of a rapidly growing boy. All I know for certain is that from birth I was exposed to influences of spirit which turned me into something new and strange which was native to Africa but not totally of it, compounded with something that made me also of Europe without being in it. And there I have always left it, without definition of myself, because the matter is doomed to be either indefinable or capable of definition only when it will

170

have been fully lived out into the answer that we are all contracted to seek at birth.

But to return to the coming of Mantis. I dwelt on his comparison with the god of the Hottentots because the myths of Heitse-Eibib which reached me simultaneously joined in a preparation of the earth on which this great seed saga of the Bushman was to fall and make prodigious growth. I deliberately call this a seed saga because I accepted intuitively, implicitly, and without any hint of doubt what I now know consciously for fact, as the circle of a long life rounds, that each of the stories which composed it carried the seed of new being and increased awareness. Why this is so I do not know. 'Why' in any case is a severely limited question, as the child discovers from the moment it begins to talk. It produces limited answers, limited as a rule to the mechanics and laws of the world, universe and life of man. But the human heart and mind come dishearteningly quickly to their frontiers and need something greater to carry on beyond the last 'why'. This beyond is the all-encompassing universe of what the Chinese called Tao and a Zen Buddhist friend, in despair over the rationalist premises native to Western man, tried to make me understand as a newly-graduated man by calling 'the great togetherness' and adding, 'in the great togetherness there are no "whys", only "thuses", and you just have to accept, as the only authentic raw material of your spirit, your own "thus" which is always so.' In and out of these great togethernesses it came to appear to me that the story brings us a sense of this unique 'so' that is to be the seed of becoming in ourselves during the time which is our lot.

This is what gives the artist in the story-teller his meaning and justification to go on telling his story, and sustains him, despite a lack of material reward or recognition, in poverty and hunger. Even though his work falls on stony ground and deaf ears or is trodden under the indifferent feet of the proliferating generations too busy to live in their frantic search for the joys and hopes of gaining the honours of the plausible world about them, this radar of the story never fails him. He does not even try to know but, through an inborn acceptance of the demands of the gift which entered him at birth, spins his story in the loom of his imagination. The life in him knows that once a story is truly told, the art which this mysterious gift places at his disposal will, when the time is ready – and the readiness is all – find listeners to take it in; their lives will be enlarged and the life even of the deaf and dumb around them will never be the same again.

This is the reason why parables are such irresistible seed stories, and the reason also, I believe, why Christ preferred to use them rather than hand out moralistic rules and recipes for human conduct. This is why, despite being the scholar he was, Christ never committed himself to writing but totally to the living word, knowing that the word that was in the beginning would transform life in a way which no written word, however inspired, could. It gives one meaning to his remark that he had come to transcend the great laws which had preceded him. This, too, was the way the first masters of Zen stretched the narrow and pointed awareness of their long troubled age in China and Japan, and so restored imagination to its pilgrim self. This is why almost the first question asked by the child after it has been fed is, 'Mother, please tell me a story', and the mother, without question, complies.

In all this we are in the presence of a great mystery which does not induce mystification but a life-giving sense of wonder out of which all that man has of religion, art and science is born. It is a cosmic area and therefore universal to man, and there is no dignified place here for presumptions like the Descartian. 'I think, therefore I am'. In the presence of this mystery at the heart of these great 'together-nesses', the human being knows how small is the area within himself where thinking is at the disposal of conscious will and preconceived purposes. He does not think so much himself but is compelled to be an instrument of life through which something beyond articulation initiates the thinking. The German language, though it may dive deeper and some-times come up muddier and less clear than the lucid French, has acquired out of this plumbing Teutonic tendency the virtue of surfacing with incomparable expressions for these great intangibles that in time move mountains of impervi-ousness. It speaks of this mystery as an *Einfall* – literally a 'fall-in' which we call 'inspiration'. One does not want to diminish the value of the word 'inspiration' since it is a reality, but it suggests something rare and privileged, whereas I believe it is as ever-present and natural to all men as breathing in and out, since it too seeks night and day to fall, as it were, into the mind and spirit; and from there it is breathed out through words, images and symbols to be transformed into behaviour. Mozart and Beethoven, if I remember rightly, use it in regard to their own work, and Beethoven wrote of how he had to dream twice of one of his most moving pieces of music before he became obedient enough to the dream to compose it. Some such elaboration, which is minimal in relation to the vast orchestration of the theme available in the history of the human spirit, is necessary, I believe, to establish the primary importance of the role of the spirit and to silence the sophisticated, watch-dog mind which raises a frantic, baying storm of alarm when any form of awareness which is not rationally, logi-cally and substantially demonstrable, approaches the door of contemporary intellect. Yet it all could still benefit, I feel, from two contemporary illustrations in depth; one basic, primitive and positive, and the other sophisticated and negative, and both significant in the process of the fermentation of Bushman yeast in my own spirit.

The first arises from a discussion I had with Jung about Bushman stories and my belief that whole civilizations had been destroyed because their stories had been taken away from them by the intrusion of a physically powerful and alien culture. At the end of an account still fresh because I had just come from the Kalahari Desert, he nodded his fine white head as the wind released a far-off refrain among the leaves of the trees he had planted as a young man at Bollingen, because they were living and viable thoughts of God to him. He went on, in that deep bass voice of his, to tell me, at great length, how his work as a healer did not take wing – the metaphor is mine – until he realized that the key to the human personality was its story. Every human being at core, he held, had a unique story and no man could discover his greatest meaning unless he lived and, as it were, grew his own story. Should he lose his story or fail to live it, he lost his meaning, became disorientated, the collective fodder of tyrants and despots, or ended up, as so many did, alienated and out of their own minds, as had the patients in the Burghölzli Asylum to whom he owed this insight and who, despite the label of madness – tied like millstones round their necks by a criminal exercise of the power of conscious conformity passing for normality – had enriched his own life and work.

Indeed he told me of such a patient, a young woman who opened his medically sound spirit to this 'fall-in' and 'insight'. He had been warned against her by the other doctors who said she had been silent for years and could be dangerous. But as he watched her – often with the sun shining from beyond the high walls of the asylum through the leaves of the trees and occasionally weaving a halo as of gold around her head – deprived of voice, his colleagues believed for ever, he could not accept that this need be so. Something in him held that she could be restored to the light of her own day. But how? One day, watching her, there came the relevant 'fall-in'. She was making certain movements, when an irresistible urge came to him to go up to her, make the same movements, close his eyes and say whatever came into his head. Obedient, he went towards her.

And here I must interrupt to add that real religious experience is not possible without a response to a glimmering of new awareness, however improbable and absurd, since it is always too mysterious and wonderful for understanding. In such a spirit of sheer obedience to the 'fall-in' Jung did just that, and as he spoke a suspicious conscious self just had time, so immediate had been his response, to suggest that he might now be provoking the dangerous reactions of which his colleagues had warned him. But to his joy he heard a low feminine voice ask: 'But how did you know?'

From that moment, contact was established and communication grew so that they could speak of her dreams.

It was sixty years later when, piloted by this deep-sea navigator we call chance, I came across her case history meticulously kept in Jung's always young hand. Already, then, dreams were used in a way that surpassed any doctrinaire Freudian or other approach to the dreaming process, and confirmed in detail his description to me of how, within six months, he could rule, despite powerful opposition from colleagues, that she should return to the sun and the world. But on her last morning before he signed the order of her release – and until then I felt I had never experienced the full meaning of 'order of release' – he called her to his office.

'Are you not anxious about going out into the world today?' he asked her solicitously.

'Of course I am,' she answered, aggressive with fearfulness.

'Did you have any dreams last night?' he asked.

'Yes, I did,' she answered, paused and added most emphatically with a good peasant adjective thrown in which I can only transcribe as 'bloody well'. 'And for once I am bloody well not going to tell you what they were.'

The expression of joy on Jung's face at this point lives with me still and his voice was a chord of music as he concluded: 'You see, at last her dreams were her own, her story was her own again.'

He told me that he was never to see her again but he heard that she had gone with the years out of their sight without need of help or treatment again from 'the likes' of him.

So here was the positive confirmation of the importance which, without my knowing it in my childhood, the story of the Bushman had for me and for my own order of release.

As for the negative illustration, it belongs inevitably to my own deprived and diminished day. When I came to telling stories myself and the years went round like the swivels of lighthouses in the dark of the main behind me, I became apprehensive about the decline of the story in its most relevant and contemporary form, and its reduction to more and more archaic expressions in the cold, brutal sensation- and action-dominated fiction starved of soliloquy and inward vision. Stories were increasingly being strung along on thin, arbitrary threads of a bleak curiosity without a twist of fantasy, feeling and wonder in their making, or, worst of all, reduced to adroit and nimble paperchases of intellect. They were written computer-wise without regard for humanity and its flesh and blood to give them life, as if all were mind – and the metamorphic spirit had no part in it. It struck me as a symptom of a deep and alarming sickness in the heart of our time, a loss of soul as the primitive companions of my boyhood would have called it, and as such an erosion of the power of increase and renewal that we and our societies so desperately needed. Where, I wondered with increasing dismay, had all the stories gone? Why this decay of the great and meaningful orchestration of the story that had occurred everywhere in the nineteenth and early twentieth centuries? What made eminent critics say complacently and with an assumption of ultimate authority, 'The novel is dead', as if it were some kind of archaic technology of the imagination, to be superseded by something more up to date? I knew writers with imaginations so bankrupt that they no longer gave birth to the characters of their stories but went to research them in the world about them. There was no metamorphosis of fiction, which is art, but rather sociological essays on people without a breath of invention or fantasy to give life to them.

In the theatre, too, where some of the greatest stories of all have been enacted, not only the people who wrote for it but also distinguished talents in the service of the story in play like the Sybil Thorndike of my early years in London, declared, 'The theatre is dead'. Critics on the subject can be discounted, in a sense, unless they are writers of stories themselves, but the alarm could not be overlooked when these symptoms appeared among considerable novelists of the day like, for example, E. M. Forster. I quote him because I knew him and had admired his sensitive, compassionate, humane and original approach to the life of his time, and always thought it tragic that what I believe was a fragmentation of spirit diminished contact between the artist in him and his natural self, and made him less creative than he could have been. I quote him, therefore, not to criticize or judge him in terms of what he could not be but strictly because I must evaluate what he said about the story on the magisterial level of the artist in him and the art to which he dedicated his life. In an essay of great merit called – with a modesty that was as admirable as it was unusual in a self-confident day – *Aspects of the Novel*, he asks the question, 'Must the novel tell a story?' and answers it to the effect that, 'Oh dear, yes, the novel must tell a story.' This answer to a vital question tells us a great deal more about E. M. Forster than the novel. He was through and through an 'Oh dear, yes' man, condemned never to be full-throated but capable at the most of 'the two cheers' of his celebrated remark: a ration of cheers, one suspects, that might have been uttered as an unenthusiastic 'Hurrah' not preceded by any 'hip-hip-hips'.

All this was brought acutely to my mind when I returned from the Second World War and saw Forster for the first time after a number of years. I went to fetch him from Benjamin Britten's home at Aldeburgh where he was already discussing the libretto for the composer's opera about Melville's Billy Budd as well as taking part in a special Festival evening. We went for a long walk on the wall beside the estuary which was the model of the water in Britten's *Curlew River*. The wall was raised above the Alde, and the marshes were still wild and abundant with natural life and not plundered as they are today, almost like the invisible scene of the scorched earth of the modern spirit made visible. It was still early summer, with the air a misty luminous yellow and the larks in such good voice that we could barely hear each other speak. He told me then he proposed reading an unfinished story of his to the Festival audience that night. I remember a strange quickening of intuition at the news and feeling hopefully, 'then the story must still live for him and this urge to tell it in public is a sign to him and all of us that it wants to be finished and lived.'

I heard the story for the first time then with increasing emotion and ended by being profoundly impressed with its significance and urgency. It was, I remember, then called 'Arctic Summer'. I said to him that I found the fragment – because it was only the prelude of a story I had heard – one of the most important things he had ever written and begged him to set everything aside and finish it.

He shook his head sadly, almost tragically, and said with an 'Oh dear' nuance in his voice: 'I shall never finish it!'

I pleaded with him then and argued through the days that followed that all who had heard it found it important and wanted it finished. More, I urged him, despite signs of growing agitation in him, it was vital to him as a man and artist to finish the story. So why, oh why not?

'I cannot,' he declared finally with an emphasis highly dramatic in a man whose disposition excluded dramatics. 'I cannot because I do not like the way it will have to finish'.

The remark for me proved both how natural stories were to him and how acute was his sense of their significance, but at the same time revealed that his awareness was inadequate for the task the story imposed on it. It had to abort the story almost as soon as its conception was assured and an advancing pregnancy diagnosed. An irresistible and an immovable force had met and a condition of self-nihilism been established. Yet I said no more. Perhaps for good or ill I realized this something was concerned with what Virgil called 'error inextricabilis', an error so profound that even some virtue can be dependent on it.

It was perhaps the explanation for why he never was more than he was. He had failed the story in him since he could not bend it to his own will and partialities. It was

179

for me accordingly a most telling illustration of the power or forces at the disposal of the story in us and how the human spirit declines when they are denied. It remains one of the most illuminating experiences on my own doorstep of time of the sort of cancer of artifice, rationalism and one-sided spirit that is denying man the fullness of his own nature and devouring the cells of renewal and re-creation that are kept alive and dynamic in him by his story, his readiness to obey the story and to add his mite to it.

And here the last word on the subject, like the first, is with the Bushman. They are words spoken by Xhabbo, the Dream, whom I have already mentioned. He was a convict – a man whom the establishment of European civilization had utterly in its power, and had not only violated his age-old right of occupation in his native land, but had also dishonoured his natural spirit, judged and punished him with the most extreme form of punishment short of death by hanging. He had been reprieved only as a result of the endeavour of that remarkable German scholar, Wilhelm Bleek. This old scholar noticed one day that Dream was sitting by himself deeply absorbed, silent and with a tragic expression on his face. Concerned, he asked what troubled him. Instantly there came from him who had never heard of, let alone known the Heidelberg and Cambridge which fathered the scholars and Forsters of this world, these words which remain for me the greatest statement ever uttered on the story. This is what Xhabbo, and the dreamer dreaming through him, said to the scholar he called master:

Thou knowest that I sit waiting for the moon to turn back for me, so that I may return to my place; that I may listen to all the people's stories . . . that I may sitting listen to the stories which yonder came, which are stories that come from a distance, for a story is like the wind,

180

it comes from a far-off quarter and we feel it. Then I shall get hold of a story . . . For I am here, I do not obtain stories; I feel that people of another place are here, they do not possess my stories. They do not talk my language . . . As regards myself I am waiting that the moon may turn back for me, that I may set my feet forward in the path, having stepped around backwards . . . I must first sit a little, cooling my arms that the fatigue may go out of them, because I sit and listen, watching for a story which I want to hear; while I sit waiting for it that it may float into my ear. I must wait listening behind me for when a man has travelled along a road and sits down he waits for a story to travel to him, following him along the same road . . . I will sit at my place, that I may listening turn backwards with my ears to my heels on which I went while I feel that a story is the wind.

Even to this day I do not know how to describe the emotions these words and the long statement that followed caused in me. It can be measured best perhaps by the fact that both the light and the shadow they cast over me have not decreased but have become more intense as I have grown older. I remember as clearly as ever the moment – how I was sitting high on my favourite perch among the broad leaves of a gigantic chinese mulberry, planted in the centre of our immense garden some seventy years before by my grandfather. It was so high, wide and dense that no one looking upwards from underneath could see me, while the view over the orchard, all aglow with peaches, apricots, plums, cherries, pears, apples, quinces, pomegranates, purple and emerald grapes, contained between long walls of spreading fig trees planted in foursomes side by side to protect the fruit from the searing air which the burning hills of summer and the hot broad vale in their keeping breathed over them, all gave me a feeling as if I and the story were part of the beginning in the Garden which our devout and constant biblical induction, let alone our instincts, would never allow us to forget.

And then instantly the tragedy implicit in the scene and the meaning in Xhabbo's statement would join forces and become too much for my self-control with a sorrow too profound for tears. The scene, of course, had to come into the mood of the moment, because its springs, and the stream of the otters, as the Bushman called it, which cut the garden in two but which also gave it the waters to nourish those alien trees and plants of Europe and China, had once made it great Bushman country. There was hardly a crest, ridge or dent in it which Klara had not endowed with some story or association with the history of her people. Yet, like the otters, the Bushman had vanished from the scene and left it as vacant and melancholy as a graveyard in which the mounds had been flattened and where only the walls remained, slowly crumbling, unattended and deconsecrated in the minds of their unnatural heirs and successors. A something without shape or name went through the calm and silence, so intense that there came to my ears a sound as of the congregation of blood singing deep within of unfailing metamorphosis to which even these broad Chinese leaves among which I sat bore witness by translation through worm into silk. The Bushman may have gone forever, but whatever it was that had made him and fashioned his spirit remained undefeated in that earth and sky.

Of course, I do not pretend that on occasions such as this – and there were many – I was capable of expressing my reaction in words such as these, but they and much else beside were there as feelings only bearable because of their potential of catharsis and transfiguration which never left me. Evidence of how active all this was within me is to be found in a story that I wrote at the age of eight after my own father died. The story, to use the term which I defined at the beginning, fell into my imagination late in September 1914, despite its preoccupation then with the shattering impact of my father's death, the outbreak at the same moment of the First World War and a civil war which divided our large family against itself. The story, moreover, dropped in to me with such force that I had to obey it despite a theme which even I feared would appear so trivial to my elders and betters that I wrote the story in secret, and to this day have never shown or spoken of it to anyone. I thereby unknowingly set the pattern which I have followed ever since: not to let the world, even its most trusted and beloved persons, sit in on what I am trying to create until I have done.

In this and many other ways the writing of that little story is perhaps the most important thing I have ever done. It was the first pilot scheme not only for my own vocation of writing, but for my general behaviour and most things of meaning to me. It marked the beginning of an awareness that one's own small contribution to creation demanded the answering of apparently insignificant, improbable and, in the eyes of the world into which I was born, totally useless calls from within the imagination. I might even say in hindsight that obedience to the private and most intimate summons of imagination is to live symbolically and religiously; not so much by rational calculation and pre-scription, much as they are needed in the service of this obedience, but as if one were following the flight of a bird. I often shudder to think what would have become of me had I not allowed the will of this intangible to take over that September morning and confer a certain 'freedom of the borough' of the here and now on me as nothing else could have done. Although there have been times when I argued that the spirit of creation is infinite and would have given me other opportunities to seize on, I believe the process of education which already had me firmly in its grip would have undermined the trust in the universal memory and instinctive knowledge of creation we bring into the world at birth and impaired my capacity to follow their improbable intimations as I obeyed them then and have tried to since.

This was my story, which needs only some explanation as to why the 'flower', at the heart of the story, meant so much to me. September is the kindest of our months. It is the beginning of spring and towards the end of the month, if the season is good, it sees the appearance of the wild freesia in the hills and rocky ridges of the native interior. Since this part is exceptionally arid, the manifestations of spring produced there are bleak and deprived compared to the eruption and violence of flower, leaf and grass in England. The appearance of this rare and beautiful flower, therefore, had a miraculous effect on all of us – young, old, white, yellow and black. It was far more beautiful than the fat, lush, multi-coloured freesias on sale in Europe. It was clean-cut in shape and clear in colour and light as a star at midnight in a moonless sky of the southern hemisphere. Only at the bottom of its cup did it hold some distillation of the blue of heaven and a suggestion of the shades befitting a herald of a dawn also in the darkness of our black earth. Its scent, which for me is still incomparable, was both more intense and more subtle than the product the horticultural-ists create in the belief that they can improve on nature. Indeed at night, when the dew began to fall, this scent would rise and travel the land and bring a sacramental quintessence to our senses. The scent combined with its

184

star-like quality to make us call the flower not freesia but by its ancient Bushman name of 'evening flower'. Perhaps for a full understanding of this impact one has to consider how harsh and demanding the soil of Africa is; how power-ful and in many ways ruthless a land it is, a giant among the continents of the globe. Yet it applies this power also to the protection of something so vulnerable and blessed as the evening flower. It explains, perhaps, as nothing else can, why we who are of Africa are bound to it and find it so great a source of wonder. It is not least of all because, even though it raises mountains to the moon, spreads outsize lakes among them, sends long rivers to the sea and rejoices in the creation of animals great and small, from the lion and elephant to the gazelle and springbok, it does not forget the fundamental significance for creation overall of the small, and the power of the minute of which the freesia with its star-light and scent of heaven at nightfall is plenipo-tentiary and which is at the heart of this stone-age matter.

As a result, throughout September my generation would scout the vast land about them for freesias, and when the first scouts returned with the news that the freesias were beginning to appear, everyone who could walk or even toddle made for the hills in the afternoon and came back in the twilight carrying bunches of freesias like phosphorescent flares in their hands. Within days of their flowering the village was perfumed all over from dusk to dawn with the smell of freesias.

In this catastrophic September of the paradoxical year of our Lord 1914, freesias were unusually late in coming. This explains perhaps why my story began with the fear of a young boy called Pierre, that no freesias would ever come again. This fear became so intense that it woke him early one morning and sent him off in haste to the hills. After a desperate search he found one sprig of freesia in bud. He

185

resisted the temptation to pick it and hastened home where he refused to say why he had been gone so long. Early the next morning, he went to visit the freesia again and already it had begun to open and spray incense on the cool air. On the second morning the one flower had been joined by two more and left only one bud to unfold. On the third morning Pierre hastened back, excited by the prospect of seeing the bloom fulfilled, only to find that an animal had stepped on and flattened it just before his arrival. The shock was so great that he began to cry, but then in the midst of crying he heard a voice saying beside him: 'Look up!'

Startled, because he had thought himself alone and abandoned, he glanced in the direction of the voice. An old Bushman with a head of mottled grey hair stood close behind him and repeated the injunction to look up. He did so, and in the precise blue of a clear September morning directly above the crushed flower a small cloud was forming.

'Your flower is there helping to make a cloud for the rains to come. It will utterly flower one day again when its cloud joins the clouds to come and the rain has been made to fall.'

I have no doubt today that the story, expressed in the symbolism which night and day urges man into an enlargement of his being through an increase of his awareness, was telling me that the disaster all around us at the time was not the end and that the flower showed how creation was always a jump or more ahead of death.

But, of course, I did not analyse the story and failed to see any connection with the fact that once it was written I had made my peace with my father's sudden death, the World War and the civil war in our midst. But I never forgot it and even found comfort in it twenty-eight years later when I was told one night in a Japanese cell in Java that I was to be executed the next morning.

However, long before that I had inklings of how my little story could have more than a subjective reality and how it had grown out of the authentic first seed of Africa in my own native and aboriginal earth. One, for instance, was a statement made to Bleek about clouds by a Bushman in the course of a discussion on death. 'The hair of our head will resemble clouds when we die . . .' he told Bleek. 'We who know, we are those who think thus, while we feel that we seeing recognize the clouds, how the clouds in this manner form themselves . . .'

The connection between crushed evening flower and its translation into cloud then seemed more like part of a message of unfailing resurrection sent straight out of the earth of Africa to all life and greatly raised my conscious appreciation of the significance of the story. Hard on this came Xhabbo's great observation on the story and its connection with the wind that is our greatest image of the spirit of creation, indeed the only one which can explain our dread over the calm which enveloped the ship of Coleridge's Ancient Mariner and the surge of hope within our hearts and minds when at the end of Valéry's finest poem, 'The Graveyard of Sailors', we hear as a reveille on a far-off bugle: 'Le vent se lève, il faut tenter vivre (The wind rises, one must try to live).'

All this combined to produce an unwavering emotion of revelation of the Pentecostal nature of the story and a full understanding why, as Xhabbo's statement to Bleek made plain, he was far more homesick for stories than for people or places. Ultimately Xhabbo needed stories more than people and implied that they were a food without which the life of his spirit would die, destroying even the unique love of life of his kind and their will to live no matter what the odds. So when I began writing my first improbable long book on a little Mediterranean island, a place which, like Xhabbo's, was not my own and where, though the time for telling stories had come at my home in Africa, I no longer 'obtained them'. Remembering this, I was back at once with Klara and my mother. In the undimmed recollection of what they told me I found unbroken the continuity between the writing my estranged grown-up self was attempting and the stories of my beginning, and the courage to work on my own unlikely and untried story.

The characters in these Bushman stories were, with rare exceptions, insects, birds and animals, and the most heroic were chosen from among the small, insignificant forms of life, alien and abhorrent to European and Bantu senses and imagination. It was impressive how the first imagination of Africa rejected the great, imposing, splendid, powerful and glittering animals from its treasury. The elephant, rhinoceros, hippopotamus, lion, leopard, baboon, the hyena indeed, figured in his stories, sometimes prominently, but, even when respected, never in the Bushman's affections and innermost imagination. It was here that his sense of purpose and energies of creation were husbanded and grew great in his sense of the infinite in the small, like that of the Blake who had seen 'infinity in a grain of sand'.

The extraordinary forms of being that populated the world of Bushman stories were part of my own life, known to me personally, almost socially, a living texture of my own imagination; the beetles, lizards, house-mice, field, short-nosed, striped and long-nosed mice; birds, like the numinous hammerkop (hammerhead) charged for the Bushman with extra-sensory perception; his 'sister the vulture'; the blue crane; 'go-away birds'; honey-guide and countless others; the bee ants, ratel (honey-badger), hare, chameleon, porcupine, jackal, rock rabbit, mongoose; the cat family among which only the lynx was an image of his love of light; the steenbok, springbok and on through the immense antelope families where his heart ranged wide and free between large and small. Though most of all he concentrated on the beloved little gazelle, the springbok, he drew into his heart and inner aspirations the gemsbok, hartebeest and above all the imperial eland, which was his and Mantis's authentic guide to ultimate metamorphosis. Subtlest, and of great transfigurative power, were elements of the sky: stars, moon, clouds, wind, particularly the great Gothic spires of whirlwinds, rain, pools of water, reeds and – of utmost significance – an image inspired by the rainbow, which he called Kwammanga and allotted to his god-hero, the Praying Mantis.

It is perhaps understandable that European invaders, confronted with such an unfamiliar, improbable and promiscuous array of characters, and their organization into patterns of myths, should have been confused and bewildered into dismissing them all as primitive nonsense. But way back in the store of European literature, after all, there is Aesop who so effectively used animals for parables of wisdom which are eloquent and persuasive to this day.

Creatures of nature can live on and dominate a world of human society as, for instance, in the stories of Beatrix Potter whose own safe passage from childhood in the claustrophobic confines of a house in London to unimpaired womanhood and marriage, was due to the pets she kept in cages in her bedroom in Kensington and the fantasies she wove round them in isolation. The role of the mouse in her *Tailor of Gloucester* first excited me as a child, because it is similar to the role of the striped mouse in one of my first Bushman stories where it, too, is an image of the hidden fecundity and infinitely detailed little forces of great powers that live in the wainscots of our cat-like consciousness.

189

They emerge only after dark and under the protective cover of the great objective unconscious to further causes of creation which can only be done in secrecy, just as the seed can only germinate in the darkness and privacy of the earth. I can think of other instances from *Alice in Wonderland* to *Black Beauty, National Velvet* and *Animal Farm*. The animals from oysters to horses and pigs are epic and seminal material of the questing imagination of man when the abstract and cerebral word fails it.

They abound, too, in folklore and fairy tales, and in Africa there are great Bantu nations who still put the soul of their people in the keeping of some animal and call themselves Men of the Crocodile, Elephant, Baboon, Duiker and so on. All these things are incontrovertible testimony to how new forms of life are not merely fresh stages in the mechanistics of zoological and botanical evolution, but each one of them a unique and truly proven achievement. They are a leap forward of spirit made visible and alive, and hence an organic and dynamic element of our being which instinct and intuition put at the disposal of the child. By maintaining continuity of origin and destination and deepening our roots in aboriginal earth they promote a growth of awareness high and wide into the blue of our own day.

One example of the leap forward of spirit demonstrated by and made accessible through the story was the tale of the beetle and two kinds of mice. An attractive young beetle woman was imprisoned by her father, the lizard, in a house in the earth. The lizard is an image of awareness bound too closely to the earth and its rocks to be good for the future. Hence the beetle woman, its future self, though also intimately of the earth, was winged, capable and desirous of taking to that other great opposite of creation, the sky. But the father, as so many fathers throughout the masculine-dominated past and present, denies the daughter, the soul

190

in him, the right to raise life towards the heavens and so fulfil the end to which it had been born.

At this point the Praying Mantis, who has appeared on Bushman earth as the instrument of ultimate meaning, has a dream and sees how life itself would be denied and arrested if the tyranny of the lizard were allowed to continue. He, therefore, sends the long-nosed mouse into battle against the lizard. We already know the reason for a mouse, but why a long-nosed mouse? Because the nose, which informs life of things not seen in the night or hidden by distance and other forms of concealment, is one of the earliest of our many images of intuition. But like all intuition, wise and sensitive as it may be, like the dove in the realities of heaven, it lacks the cunning of the serpent which is necessary to overcome the lizard. Inevitably the long-nosed mouse is killed by the lizard and, though followed by countless gallant long-nosed kinsmen, all are killed and the lizard remains an adamant and triumphant impediment to 'becoming' new being. Happily, Mantis is informed of the disaster in a dream and decides to send the striped mouse into battle instead. The striped mouse, of course, has a sensitive nose but it is not too long, there is no hubris of intuition, and its stripes are of even greater significance. They are the outward signs that it is a more differentiated form of being and consciousness. Just as Odysseus was chosen to complete our Homeric quest, not because he was the bravest and wisest of the men who fought on the great plain of Troy, but because he combined without exaggeration in one person the best elements of all, so the striped mouse is elected as a stone-age kind of Odysseus, to battle for the future of all. He kills the lizard, calling out as he does so, 'I am killing by myself to save friends', and hastens to free the beetle woman, the feminine in life, all in a manner I described in *The Heart of the*

Hunter. All the dead forces of intuition, the long-nosed mice, are resurrected, and there follows a most moving description of how this army of tiny visionary creatures is led back to the palace of the Praying Mantis, the stone-age's supreme image of the infinite in the small. Jubilant and triumphant, they follow the striped mouse and the beetle woman marching at his side, feeling herself 'to be utterly his woman'. As they march, they wave high above their heads like flags the fly whisks which the Bushman of the great plains of the south alone had made out of animal tails.

It was for me, hearing this again and again, as though the earth joined in this triumphant waving like a kind of hosanna, not uttered but enacted. It was, and remains all the more so, because the story ends with the Mantis bringing up the rear, suddenly seeing that the wind has risen and everywhere the long, tasselled, green-gold grass is waving too. And this wind, I was told, came out of the east, the east where the new days are born. Seeing all this, Mantis leaned back, content because he had 'foreseen it all in a dream'.

Alone in the imagery of the stories told to me, Mantis was dealt with in epigrammatic form without extended definition because I was young and too affected by this tale. As a result, nothing more was necessary to underscore his importance in the rich mixture of stories poured on me like those splendours, the dreams of Caliban of the Island at the still centre of the storm in *The Tempest*. But this much and this approach were necessary to explain why the Bushman stories held me as no European fairy-tale did, though I came to love them too. The wolf, the fox, the bear, the giants, the bean-stalk, the sleeping beauties, the chocolate-box princesses and princes, came into my imagination at a more conscious level because they came later and were

192

hearsay material to me. For me, the characters of the Bushman stories were all a direct part of the processes of growing
up. Isolated from the great tides of civilization ebbing and
swelling like the seas over Asia and Europe, the Bushman
fought the battle for light and creation in his own triumphant way, transforming darkness into light and as he
renewed and increased himself, he held back the forces that
sought to deny life, until European and Bantu man arrived
to quench him. Considering how long that old, old Africa
had been there, a known unknown, a mystery in the full
sun, and that none of the great civilizations surrounding it
had been able to penetrate its natural frontiers and explore
it, one would have thought this achievement alone would
have entitled the Bushman to respect and been a passport
to human consideration by the invaders. Yet despite all this,
there appears to have been something just in what he was
which provoked all that was worst in the invaders and
aroused the extreme selfrighteousness which can only be
justified by the unconscious guilt for the wounds man
inflicts on himself. It resulted in this compulsion to kill in
the illusion that he would only have to remove the external
reminders of this primordial unrest to calm his conscience
forever. It was all summed up for me in the cry of explanation that both white and black sent echoing, like the
voice of Cain, down the canyons of the centuries: 'You see.
He just would not tame!'

What, then, was this hated being? It is too late, I think,
to answer this question decently and in the round. It is, in
any case, something so profound and so remote from what
we have become ourselves that no answer, perhaps, would
ever have been complete. We would have been able to do
better, however, had our ancestors paused before the killing
to ask themselves the question and then looked, for
instance, into what it was in the Bushman spirit that made

him cover the rock of his native land with paintings of the external world and the world within him, covering all the aspects of art which the visual artists of the great cultures had explored: everything from the world about him, insect, animal and human, historical and immediate to his innermost world and his aspirations towards a meaning and reality beyond his here and now. It is so inspired and moving that it raises his painting to the order of that of an unusually articulate civilization.

We have incontrovertible evidence today that he was already painting superbly some thirty thousand years ago, so that by the time Europeans and Bantu invaded his country they had everywhere Louvres and National Galleries of paintings, still glowing with enough colour and light to brighten the darkest shadows of overhang and cave. Nor did the newcomers listen to their stories and music which made the Bushman dance to the moon and under the stars and act out the meaning to come as it stirred within him and in the process gain access to those transfigurative energies which had entered him at conception. Luckily I was somewhat better placed. My family had over three centuries' experience of him, even though mostly only in battle; had been puzzled by him, which was a beginning, however slight. It started a process of wonder which two little Bushmen, Klara, the Bleeks and Lucy Lloyd augmented to put me in closer touch with his spirit. Moreover, after the Second World War, I saw something of the original version still being lived in the central Kalahari and had a sufficient glimpse of his unique being to suggest some of the answers.

The essence of this being, I believe, was his sense of belonging: belonging to nature, the universe, life and his own humanity. He had committed himself utterly to nature as a fish to the sea. He had no sense whatsoever of property, owned no animals and cultivated no land. Life and nature

194

owned all, and he accepted without question that, provided he was obedient to the urge of the world within him, the world without, which was not separate in his spirit, would provide. How right he was is proved by the fact that nature was kinder to him by far than civilization ever was. This feeling of belonging set him apart from us on the far side of the deepest divide in the human spirit. There was a brief moment in our own great Greek, Roman, Hebraic story when his sort of being and our own were briefly reconciled, and Esau, the first-born, the hunter, kissed and forgave his brother Jacob, the strangely chosen of God, for his betrayal. But after that Esau, like Ishmael before him, vanishes from our story, and a strange longing hidden in some basement of the European spirit still waits with increasing tension for his return. Meanwhile, the divide in our consciousness between the Esau and the Jacob in man deepened, and the stone-age hunter and his values could not have been more remote and antagonistic to ours when we clashed increasingly in southern Africa. We were rich and powerful where he was poor and vulnerable; he was rich where we were poor, and his spirit led to strange water for which we secretly longed. But, above all, he came into our estranged and divided vision, confident in his belonging and clothed as brightly as Joseph's coat of dream colours in his own unique experience of life. Where we became more and more abstracted and abstract, he drew closer to feeling and the immediacy of instinct and intuition. Indeed for him, his feeling values were the most important and the liveliest. Even the language he spoke was a feeling language, expressing reality not in ideas, calculation and abstraction so much as through the feelings provoked in him. He would speak of how the sun, feeling itself to be sitting prettily in the sky and feeling itself to be warm, believed it could make people on the cold earth feel warm as well. His language, therefore, was poetic rather than realistic, and, although he was not indifferent to a robust range of the sort of verbs we favour, all usages of his grammar, still warm from the presses of his aboriginal imagination, were contained in an assessment of reality and meaning through feeling.

This pre-eminence of feeling for natural forms of life was attached to him from birth. The family became his fundamental social and universal unit, and his feeling of belonging was so wide and deep that all on earth and in the universe were family to him. It was the unchanging rod in his bureau of standards by which experience of reality and a sense of future were measured. He seemed to have felt no need to organize himself into tribes or nations. He moved naturally as hunter societies do, in small family groups, and his contact with others of his own kind appears to have been unusually free of friction and dominated by the consideration that they were a family among other human families and, one and all, they were part of a universal family.

He was never imperilled as we are by numbers and the blurring of the human spirit which their collective standards and approximations exact today. He had as a result no national organizations or institutions, no ruling establishment and therefore no kings, queens or presidents. The highest and noblest titles he could bestow were those of 'grandfather' and 'grandmother'. And since the stars, with which the nights of the southern hemisphere are so densely packed that one can hear them straining at the seam of the Milky Way in the stillness, since they were family too, he naturally addressed the greatest of them as grandfather and grandmother, since there was no discrimination of value and dignity between the sexes. Two of the brightest, for instance, Canopus and Sirius, were female stars, and since both were associated with one of his delicacies, the white-ant larvae referred to by my ancestors as Bushman rice, he would encourage and warm them from the cold with some of his own positive fire. For instance, he would call on a child, 'Give me yonder piece of wood, that I may put the end of it in the fire, that I may point it burning towards grandmother, for grandmother is carrying Bushman rice.'

Hungry, they would call on one of them. 'Thou shalt give me thy heart, with which thou dost sit in plenty: thou shalt take my heart with which I am desperately hungry, that I may also be full like thee.'

As important as the element of belonging was the feeling of being known. Perhaps this more than anything else sets him apart from us and the rest of Africa. In this connection we must not forget that the great black societies of Africa, from which we derive our notions of the primitive, were and are not primitive at all. They were already extremely advanced in what we like to term the stages on the way to civilization; they, too, were people of property, with sophisticated concepts of life, law, order and makeshift ideological abstractions of their own. Moreover, they had already succumbed to the heresy of numbers and inflicted on themselves the stifling collective priorities in which socialism and communism are now trying to imprison the life of our time, as if they were the newest leap forward instead of a lethal somersault backwards into an amply discredited pattern of spirit.

Relatively, of course, they have not gone down the road of cosmic anonymity and unbelonging as far as we have done, thanks to the great natural world that still contains and restrains them, but far enough nonetheless to hate stone-age man with a vehemence as great if not greater than our own. They, too, have tended to lose, as we ourselves with rare, individual exceptions have totally lost, this sense of being known. How many of us, for instance, have any

197

emotional understanding of what St Paul meant by his conclusion of what is for me the greatest statement, not excluding Dante's, ever made on love: 'Now we see through a glass, darkly; but then face to face: now I know in part; but then shall I know even as also I am known' (I *Corinthians*)?

We have become perhaps the most bigoted collection of know-all cultures and sects the world has ever seen, but this sense of being known, which accompanied, uplifted and preserved the Bushman from extremes and held him accountable throughout his thousand and one centuries alone in the vastness of Africa, has vanished from the heart of modern man. All that Klara told me, all I read, and all I experienced of the Bushman in the years I knew him in his last keep in the heartland of the Kalahari, almost overwhelmed me with nostalgia for this shining sense of belonging, of being known and possessing a cosmic identity of one's own, recognized by all from insect to sun, moon and stars which kept him company, so that he felt he had the power to influence them as they influenced and helped him. All was two-way traffic and honourable reciprocity. I have already anticipated some of this obliquely in the story of the Morning Star and his response to the appearance of Canopus and Sirius, the grandmother stars, in his night sky but there was more of this in the practical detail of his everyday life.

For instance, as a hunter he would call on the stars to guide the hand that released the arrow from his bow, with a certainty that was as much a command as a prayer: 'Thou shalt take my arm with which I do not kill, for I miss my aim. Thou shalt give me Thine arm.' He already knew himself well enough to be in battle against error and fallibility and falsehood in himself and to turn to the cosmic pattern of stars and constellations, in ordered courses where

198

falsehood and error did not exist, to overcome his own inadequacies.

In fact, one of my most moving memories is concerned with just this aspect of his life in the Kalahari. One evening I went from my camp fire in the central desert to see if all was well with a little Bushman group, desperate for food and water, that I had encountered that day. As I came near their own fire, my Bushman guide and closest companion stopped me. Against the clear starlight I saw the outline of a woman and, as my eyes became more accustomed to the dark, noticed that she was holding her baby, a boy, high above her head and calling softly to the sky above.

I asked my guide what she was doing. Reproving me for not speaking more softly, he whispered: 'She is asking the stars up there to take from her son the heart of a child and give him the heart of a star instead.'

'But why the heart of a star?' I asked.

'Because the stars are great hunters,' he answered with the condescension which my ignorance of what was essential and self-evident to him always provoked. 'And she wants them to give him the heart of a hunter too. If you listen carefully you will hear the sounds of their hunting cries up there.'

I listened and indeed a far sea-sound came from the stars to my ears.

'You hear!' he whispered. 'How they are calling out "Tssa!" and "Tssk!"'

These sounds needed no explanation. For generations all of us in Africa had used and were still using these very words to set our dogs after game. I had thought until then that they were of our own invention. But that evening I knew we had them from the Bushman and he had them from the stars. The word that was in the beginning came from the stars and the word was true.

199

That, of course, was more evidence of his intimacy and assumption of two-way communication with his universe long before this inbuilt pattern in life was revealed through the dream of a ladder pitched between another desert and heaven to a Jacob who had done a hunter and brother wrong. It is testimony, however, that should be amplified by the fact that the sun, too, made a sound for him, the same great ringing sound it made for Goethe and which he asserts as fact in the 'Prologue in Heaven' in *Faust Part I*.

As long as the Bushman heard this sound of the sun and stars and could include it in the reckoning of his spirit, all was well in his world, but when the sound ceased, tragedy was upon him. It needed only one death, so clear was his identity, so at one with the family over all, that the sun ceased ringing and a star fell.

To use his own words, 'Since the feeling strings were cut, the sun has ceased to ring for me in the sky.' His heart cried out specifically on the death of a friend because that is what the cutting of strings meant; or more generally: 'When our hearts fall down, that is the time when the star also falls down. When the star feels that our hearts fall over, as when something that has been standing upright falls over on its side – for the stars know the time at which we die – the star tells the other people who do not know that we have died.'

And the wind, the spirit that travels the world and time, would know it too, and, in the case of the precision and the symbolism of truth which presided over his spirit, would join in to perform the final rite on behalf of life that the man had served so well: 'The wind does this when we die,' he declared. 'Our own wind blows, for we who are human beings, we possess wind, we make clouds when we die. Therefore the wind makes dust because it intends to blow, taking away our footprints, with which we had walked about, while we still had nothing the matter with us, and our footprints which the wind intends to blow away would otherwise still be plainly visible. The thing would seem as if we still lived. Therefore the wind intends to blow, taking away our footprints.'

So even at the exit of the world his spirit stood whole and fast, demanding accuracy in the last account with life and, compared to the longing for immortality which characterizes Western man, without complaint or regret. Indeed the hunger for immortality of the ego, too, had to preserve the proportions of creation and it plays the ultimate role as an instrument of truth and not as an impediment and source of confusion. Like rebirth and resurrection, death, oblivion and the wind were people of the early race, dark sisters who had their place among the first family of life at nightfall by his little fire with its spire of flame reaching up towards their cousins, the sun, moon and all the other stars.

For years I would watch the Bushman as I shall always remember him by countless such fires at nightfall, so confident and at home in his immense wasteland, full of an unappeasable melancholy. He was the Esau being we daily betrayed in our partial and slanted modern awareness, and instead of blaming ourselves for the betrayal, we projected it on to him to such an extent that we had to kill him as Cain killed Abel. Yet, though he himself is vanishing fast from the vision of our physical senses as Esau vanished from the great story which contained as it fashioned the foundations of our culture, he lives on in each one of us through an indefinable guilt that grows great and angry in some basement of our own being. The artist and the seer, even though the priests who should have known it best have forgotten it for the moment, know there is an Esau, a first man, a rejected pattern of being within us which is personified by something similar to a Bushman hunter,

201

without whom they cannot create and sustain a vision of time fulfilled on which a life of meaning depends.

As they create and dream their dreams by making his sort of being contemporary, by linking that which was first with what is new and latest and all that is still to come, they do work of cosmic importance and in the process are invaded with a compassion for this betrayed Esau element that leads unerringly to a love that is overall and which knew him long before we were made. Like that which created creation, named or not named, known or unknown, he is always there.

That this vital link with the first man in us is no subjective assumption of mine but objective truth is proved, I believe, by the striking parallels that exist between the basic images of his spirit and those of Shakespeare, Goethe, Blake and Valéry on which I have already drawn. I know of many more. But I believe these are enough to show how, in considerations such as these, we can proceed to dispel the lethal imperviousness in the cultures which compelled men to fear and extinguish him. Our diminishing civilizations can only renew themselves by a reconciliation between two everlasting opposites, symbolized by Cain and Abel, Jacob and Esau and, in our own day, by the Bushman and his murderer. We have no excuse left for not seeing how fatally divided against themselves the processes of civilization have been, and how horrific the consequences in the human spirit. Now there is only a re-dedication of man to knowing himself, the command of both Christ and Apollo, which can lead him to rediscover the wholeness lost in the beginning in a contemporary and greater form. Something of this sort is the armour the spirit needs for a future imperilled by corruption from the power we have acquired over the forces of nature. Since this future has come to include man's journey to the stars, the proportions that our humanity needs to protect it from brutalization by hubris of power and extremes of greed demand that we should look back to the moment the first man summoned his son, his future self, and gave him a stick alight with his fire, his awareness, and pointed it to a great feminine star, a mother figure through which an overall father begets. In that slight exercise of what the anthropologists label stone-age superstition, the journey to space was born and made inevitable, and we have an inkling why the first man thought of the glittering men of heaven as hunters.

The hunter in the Bushman family, of course, was the person who provided the food needed for physical survival. But it is of fundamental importance to remember that for him spirit and matter were manifestations of one another and the well-being of the body and the heart ultimately one. It was an axiom of his being that he could not eat without participating also in the character of the essential spirit he attributed to the source of his food. A Bushman father, therefore, would as soon as possible feed his son on the heart of a leopard, the bravest of the brave in the animal kingdom, so that his son would become brave and, as he put it, 'possess the heart of a leopard too'.

There presided always over his eating a sacramental element. His spirit was naturally so transubstantiative that he did not deny the animal reciprocity in the matter. In one of his most moving stories, like all great tales a frontier story and as illuminating and enigmatic as an early *Hamlet*, he tells of a lion who seeks to become a man. For this purpose a lion, significantly on his way to life-giving water, encounters a young hunter whom he overpowers and fixes firmly in the fork of a thorn tree with the intention of eating him when he has drunk his fill of the desert water of life. The young hunter, unknown to the lion, is merely pretending to be dead. Hurt by the rough fork of the tree, the pain forces tears to start from his eyes. Amazed, the lion licks away the tears with a strange tenderness and in that instant the relationship of lion and man is transformed and takes wing. It is as if the suffering of the young man is absorbed and understood by the lion and is translated into a compassion which establishes a bond between them that demands their union alive or dead. Sadly, as the story makes clear, it is a reckoning so royal, of such ultimate individuation and so transcendent a value that neither the community of the young hunter nor the young man himself, nor indeed the king of the greatest animal kingdom on earth, can yet achieve it.

In this, as in all else, the hunter for the stone-age man was the image, the personification of the greatest of all the urges of his being, the hunger for food of the spirit, for meaning that would transfigure him. He felt himself without doubt or self-questioning a participant in the hunt that was on everywhere, not only on earth but in the expanding universe above and about him. The hunter was charged with the supreme image of all within himself that sought a truth that would transcend everything and quiet the unrest and the hunger for a reality beyond his here and now, his tiny allotment of time and space. He already knew instinctively what Baudelaire came to recognize at the end of one of his finest poems, 'Les Phares' [The Lighthouses], one of the most moving surveys of the meaning of the art of painting that I know. 'What is art, o lord, what is this ardent sob that breaks out and re-echoes from age to age?' he asks with a cry of anguish at the end of the poem and concludes that it is also, 'A summons from hunters lost in the great woods'. This symbolic hunter was the Bushman's summons, the pentecostal element at the quick of his being that connected him to a process of becoming something other and more than he was in his given moment, always seeking to increase himself through his painting, story-telling, dreaming the great dream over all, making music and dancing his dances in sacred circles under the stars and the moon. And although I mention his music and dancing last, they were perhaps his most immediate way of linking himself to creation and the forces that raised the sun out of darkness; the stars and moon out of a bright day that blotted them out, so restoring them to the night that renews and reveals them in their lawful courses.

I was privileged to encounter the Bushman at a time when his culture was sufficiently whole to have preserved his music and dancing relatively intact and I marvelled at how, despite the diversity I uncovered in his highly differentiated stories, in the music and dancing from north to south, east to west, he was at one and his culture united and whole. Long after his story-tellers and painters had vanished from my part of Africa, fragments of his dancing and music remained. His last survivors had only to take a few dancing steps, utter a refrain or two for them to declare, with tears beyond our understanding springing to their eyes, as Klara and two little grey-haired old men had declared after a rehearsal of their history performed for me one unforgettable evening in the interior, 'But ah! How we have become young again'.

The steps and the music stayed with me so clearly that I recognized them forty years later as part of the patterns of the dances and the singing of Kalahari men. The dances were of all kinds but there were three that had a special meaning for me. There was first of all the dance of the little hunger that was performed to express the Bushman's need of food in his struggle for physical survival, and to enlist the help of the stars that knew no falsehood or evasion but were always accurate and true. This was the dance that had its fulfilment in another performed to express gratitude to the animal which had allowed itself to be killed so that he could live. And there was the dance of the great hunger, not for the meat of fruit of the earth but for the food which the hunter within and his fellow hunters, the stars, were after. I suspect that this was the grand dance of which my ancestors spoke, the dance which fascinates the anthropologist of today almost to the exclusion of all other forms of his dancing: it is called the trance dance. This was the dance in which one of the dancers who had a gift of healing,of dreaming great dreams, of seeing visions and was, accordingly, a seer and prophet to his clan, summoned power, as it were, from the universe to reinforce his gift from life of healing the sick and anguished among his kind.

I have seen such a person also acquire similar powers and perform his healing in lesser dances, but in this dance of dances an awesome element and power was acquired that was not present in the others. It, too, was performed in a circle of mushroom magic, the image of mathematical completion, the sacred mandala of Tibet and the total rounding of the torn and divided soul which the modern psychologist tries to achieve in depth. It was danced like all the others, by the men, the women sitting close to the wavering margin of firelight, leaning against the black of night and providing the rhythm with song and clapping of hands while the dancers added to the beat by the pounding of their feet in the scarlet Kalahari sand and the swish of the rattles tied round their ankles. But it went on much longer than any others. In fact, the last great dance I saw in the Kalahari in 1954 started at about four on an afternoon of clouds raised like temples in a sky illuminated with the revelation of lighting, and ended only at about midnight when the first heavy drops of rain began to fall. From time to time, one of the older women would jump up and break into the sacred circle to urge the men to greater exertion, until at the climax, as I watched it alone and apart in the dark, the whole of nature seemed to come alive and join in the dance and its call on the universe to appease a terrible hunger. The thunder became incessant, the lions suddenly began to roar, the ostriches to boom, the night plover to pipe its deep-sea call, the hyenas to howl and the jackals to bark as if they were a chorus of fate sent to swell the music and the prayer for appeasement and wholeness. The beat of feet, hands, and voice indeed became so loud and regular that it was like that of a great time machine, and heard out of context on my taped recordings today, the beat sounds not so much human as like enormous pistons driving a ship at full speed ahead. At this moment the healer chose to lay his hands on the sick, pressing them tight against the ailing bodies before pulling them along and up to the top of the aching heads, uttering, as the hands left them, the defiant cry of the animal spirit with which the sickness was associated. At that moment the music would change; the frenzy left it and a mood of the most tender and delicate compassion took over, as if one and all knew instinctively what Paracelsus, the Einstein of modern medicine, as he has been called, knew in the sixteenth century when he declared that without love and compassion there could be no healing.

At that moment I realized why the dance had to last so long: fatigue was to the healer what drugs are to the psychiatrist – a means of lowering the level of consciousness and its wilful inhibitions so that the unconscious forces and the instinctive powers at the disposal of all life could rise unimpeded and be released in the healer. What these forces are I cannot define and would not be so foolish as to try to describe by anything save their consequences. Judging by those, they were as great as they were dangerous, and only that prolonged and highly disciplined ritual of the dance could first contain and then transform them into elements of healing. The danger, of course, was greatest for the healer. He was the lightning conductor to the great storm of primeval energies which had been released, and when the healing was accomplished he fell unconscious to the earth. Another dance and cycle of song began to bring him back to the here and now from this underworld of the forces which he had plumbed and released in order to heal. When he opened his eyes at last and the water from a dozen or more ostrich eggshells was poured down his parched throat, the look on his face in that firelight was, I believe, the oldest I have ever seen on a human being, and the expression that of a pilgrim who could never tell others where and how far he had travelled that night.

Yet despite all this, he did not bleed at the nose. I mention this because on many rock paintings of dancers the healers are depicted as faint and bleeding profusely at the nose, as if to demonstrate the Greek healers' dictum, 'only the wounded physician heals'. I can only vouch that at the end of the dance I understood why wholeness and being holy were one and the same, just as I and all around me that night on earth and in heaven had felt to be one. And somehow whenever I think of his dancing and how it renewed and made him whole, I recall a dance I witnessed when his culture was intact. It was a dance to the full moon, a moon as beautiful as any moon of Japan. When I asked them why they performed that dance, they said with pity at my ignorance: 'The moon is about to fall away and shall utterly die unless we show her by our dancing how we love her not a little; how we feel we want her to live, utterly knowing that feeling thus, she will not die but return, lightening the night for our feet on which we go out and return.' In all these and many other ways, out of his belonging and being known, he felt responsible to the universe and capable

208

even of influencing its course. Feeling thus, he was preserved from that erosion of meaning and sense of participation in the wider plan of creation which is eating out the heart and will to be and to become of our bright technological day.

For all these and many other reasons, when I returned from nearly a decade of war, I thought it well worthwhile to make one last effort to preserve the Bushman and his culture in the heart of what I called the lost world of the Kalahari, and try to arrest there this age-old story of persecution and annihilation. I persuaded the British Government for the first time in our history to appoint an officer charged with the sole duty of learning the Kalahari Bushman's language, and to live with him and get to know, understand and defend him. I did not mean to imply thereby that he should be preserved as some kind of living museum piece. I had too great a respect for him and his potential for creative re-evaluation. All I wanted was recognition of his humanity, his values that were, at their best, precious qualities that we had neglected in ourselves and at our peril, and his right to native land wherein his security was guaranteed so as to give him time enough to find a way of his own into the world of the future. 'Give this officer fifty years with them,' I told a sympathetic administration, 'and at the end of that time ask him for some recommendation on how to go on from there.'

But I did not mean to leave it at that. I had experienced a Kalahari Desert that had overflowed its arbitrarily imposed political boundaries from South West Africa which today goes by the unhistorical and utterly contrived name of Namibia, and up and over the river boundaries of Angola right to the outskirts of Mossamedes itself. All this vast area was still recognizable stone-age country, and the Bushman hunter's life still a relatively coherent culture. Moreover, this land was a desert only in the sense that it had no permanent surface water and was covered with grass, shrubs, trees, bush, even forest, a dense life-giving vegetation that made it the home of a rich and abundant animal population. Yet at that moment it had no great and lasting economic value in the modern sense.

So I had a dream of persuading all the governments who claimed sovereignty over this immense tract to join forces and declare it an international heritage, transforming it into a unique reserve where both the first man and his attendant animal world would be protected and conserved. I began working at once with my friends to that end, but we had begun too late. The world of Empire, which had this unique and precious earth in its keeping, collapsed, and the forces of an archaic nationalism moved in to take its place. In the process, the Bushman was once more overlooked and his claims forgotten. He was not physically eliminated, but merely overwhelmed by a brash new world wherein he not only had no voice in his own future but had no command of any language which would have made sense to the powers that seized his secluded land in a cast-iron grip. Moreover, he had no immunities whatsoever to protect him against an infected world, sick with unschooled power and uncritical worship of its technological and material endowments. As a result, when I went back recently, as I felt I had to in order to see what, if anything, could still be done to help him, I hardly recognized the man I had known in the nineteen fifties among the tragic fragments of families left behind like flotsam and jetsam on some desert island beach by the tidal wave of the mindless forces we had released and allowed to sweep over it.

As a result, he was being destroyed rapidly and more subtly now from within himself. To use his own metaphor, I found that his story had been utterly taken away from

210

him. He could no longer live it and had only a fast-receding memory of it left in the labyrinthine regions of his convulsed imagination, like an echo of the brave voice of the legendary hunter pausing to call farewell at the edge of his forest of the night before vanishing on his quest for the great white bird of truth. His culture was dying before our eyes, and he and what was left of it were about to vanish physically and spiritually into the bastard bloodstream of his unworthy conquerors. No doubt he will live on as other vanished and unrecorded men live on, and add a nuance or two to the being of the future, a look in the eye, a curl of hair, a tone of affirmative and indestructible laughter, a quickening of fantasy and expression on some face, that will stir men to wonder and to experience an inexplicable nostalgia of the heart and provoke a dream of new-old life in their sleep. This could be reward and treasure of an incorruptible kind. However, the horror of it for the moment was, to use a phrase I had learned out of the heart of suffering of Japan, 'an unbearable of life one had to bear'. There was nothing else to be done; neither he nor I and others who wished him well had any court or power in the world to whom we could appeal in our so-called enlightened day. The organizations that should have been the first to rush to his aid, like that whited-sepulchre of the hopes which had sustained us in yet another world war in which the best of my generation died, the United Nations, would not heed and had no ear for the voice of so tiny and powerless a minority, as it has had no ear for the hapless Indians of central America, Brazil, and other violated natural worlds.

Ironically, the much condemned apartheid country of South Africa was alone inclined to listen and concede the Bushman a certain recognition of identity and rights of his own. Far from perfect as that recognition is, it is more than

211

anything practised by the apprentices to the nationalism fathered by the political liberalism which is the international fashion and dominant hypocrisy of our day. All we could do who had gone to the Kalahari to testify to the Bushman's human and primordial right to a pursuit of life, liberty and happiness in his own way, was to persuade dying fragments of his culture to re-enact for us such memory as they had of what I ventured at the beginning to call a stone-age civilization. Added to the film record, *The Lost World of the Kalahari*, which I made in 1954–55, my book of the same title and its sequel, *The Heart of the Hunter*, and the film I made in 1982 with Paul Bellinger and Jane Taylor, *Testament to the Bushmen*, what I have written here is in a sense, therefore, a last will and testament. Late, partial and hurried as it was in the doing, it will make those who ponder its fragmentary bequests nonetheless rich because they are all he had left to bequeath of the wealth of natural spirit out of which in his own day he gave so abundantly with all the grace, willingness and fulness of which he in his time on earth was capable.

For myself, I can only record that on my last return from the desert my own world had never seemed bleaker. For not only was the sense of belonging and being known absent, but the individual self which was an instinct of his being and centre of his totality of imagination and doing was everywhere under powerful attack.

First man, as I knew him and his history, was a remarkably gentle being, fierce only in defence of himself and the life of those in his keeping. He had no legends or stories of great wars among his own kind and regarded the killing of another human being except in self-defence as the ultimate depravity of his spirit. I was told a most moving story of how a skirmish between two clans, in which just one man was killed on a long-forgotten day of dust and heat and sulphur sun, caused them to renounce armed conflict forever. He was living proof to me of how the pattern of the individual in service of a self that is the manifestation of the divine in man was built into life at the beginning and will not leave him and the earth alone until it is fulfilled. It is no mere intellectual or ideological concept, however much that, too, may be needed, but a primary condition written into the contract of life with the creator.

As I thought of the first man's instinctive sense for the meaning of life, I seemed to be more aware than ever of the loneliness creeping into the heart of modern man because he no longer sought the answers of life with the totality of his being. He was in danger of going back precisely to those discredited collective concepts and surrendering this precious gift of being an individual who is specific for the sake of the whole, an individual who believes that a union of conformity is weakness but that a union of diversities, of individuals who are different and specific, is truly strength. A grey, abstract, impersonal organization of a materialistic civilization seemed to be pressing in on us everywhere and eliminating these life-giving individual differences and sources of enrichment in us. Everywhere men were seeking to govern according to purely materialistic principles that make us interesting only in so far as we have uses. It was true even in Zululand, let alone Paris and London.

I was speaking once to an old Zulu prophet who, when I asked him about their First Spirit, Umkulunkulu, said to me: 'But why are you interested in Umkulunkulu? People no longer talk about him. His praise names are forgotten. They only talk about things that are useful to them.'

This ancient reverence for the individual, so clear and unprovisional in the Bushman, has been lost; this individual dedicated to a self that is greater than the individual, who serves something inside himself that is a microcosm of the great wheeling universe. This individual who, by being his self, is in a state of partnership with an overwhelming act of creation and is thereby adding something to life that was not there before, is being taken away from us. We no longer feel the longing, the wonder and the belonging out of which new life is raised. In the depths of ourselves we feel abandoned and alone, and therein is the sickness of our time.

Human beings can enjoy anything except a state of meaninglessness, of which it seems a great tide is creeping down upon us. Apparently nothing but conformity will do. Take, for instance, the concept we hear so much about – the statistical notion of the average man. When you come to think about it, there is no such thing as an average man. It is like the average rainfall, which never falls. But because numbers have replaced unique and human considerations in the faceless abstractions of our time, we feel lost in a world where nobody cares any more for what we are in ourselves. Inevitably we cease to care in return. One of the most awful consequences is that, as we lose touch with the natural man within, which demands a unique self of us, we lose respect for him. And as the natural man within loses honour, so too does nature without. We no longer feel reverence for nature, and defoliation of spirit and landscape are everywhere to be seen.

It is only now that we have lost what I re-found in the Kalahari in the nineteen fifties when, for months on end, I moved through the country no 'sophisticated' man had ever set eyes on, that I realize in full what it meant and did for my own senses, brutalized by years of war. It was as if I had been in a great temple or cathedral and had a profound religious experience. I returned to the world knowing that, unless we recover our capacity for religious awareness, we will not be able to become fully human and find the self that the first man instinctively sought to serve and possess.

Fewer and fewer of us can find it any more in churches, temples and the religious establishments of our time, much as we long for the churches to renew themselves and once more become, in a contemporary idiom, an instrument of pentecostal spirit. Many of us would have to testify with agonizing regret that, despite the examples of dedicated men devoted to their theological vocation, they have failed to give modern man a living experience of religion such as I and others have found in the desert and bush. That is why what is left of the natural world matters more to life now than it has ever done before. It is the last temple on earth which is capable of restoring man to an objective self wherein his ego is transfigured and given life and meaning without end.

Looking back with a nostalgia that I am powerless to describe and which often wakes me aching in the night and walks like my own shadow at my side, I must testify with all the power and lucidity of expression at my command that this lost world was one of the greatest of such temples, in which the first man and the animals, birds, insects, reptiles and all, had a glow upon and within them as if they had just come fresh and warm from the magnetic fringes of whoever made them. He and they were priests and acolytes of this first temple of life, and the animals dominated his stories, his art, his dancing and imagination because they followed neither their own nor his will but solely that of their creator.

Follow, I would add today, the first man in ourselves, as well as the rainbow pattern of beasts, birds and fish that he weaves into the texture of the dreams of a dreaming self, and we shall recover a kind of being that will lead us to a self where we shall see, as in a glass, an image reflected of the God who has all along known and expected us.

This is as far as my own words about my experience of

215

the being of the Bushman can carry me and yet there is more. The Word that was at the beginning and shall be at the end is a living word. The living word and the living truth are always more than statistics and facts. Neither can be imprisoned in any particular expression of themselves however valid and creative, but must move on as soon as that phase of themselves is fulfilled. The concepts, cultures, whole civilizations, indeed, are not terminals, but wayside camps, pitched at sunset and broken at dawn so that they can travel on again. As end and beginning round to meet in my own life, there seems only one lasting form without inbuilt obsolescence of any kind in which their nature can be conveyed from generation to generation, and that is through the story. And it is in a great Bushman story that I sought and found refuge from the sense of doom of the Bushman idiom of primitive man that assailed me on my return to one of our cities where, to use Xhabbo's words, 'I no longer obtained stories'.

It is a story which is, in a sense, like a symphony wherein many notes and chords are struck on a diversity of instruments to compose a whole. I must begin the story, therefore, with a description of the characters and elements that are the instruments, the notes and chords and associations. Thus pre-auditioned in imagination, when the full orchestra is assembled, the key and scale determined, the listeners' minds will be wide open to the subtle alchemical intent of the story.

The principal character in such a seminal story, of course, is Mantis. The others that appear in it are Kwammanga, who is described on this occasion as Mantis's son-in-law; Kwammanga's son; Kwammanga's shoe-piece; and Mantis's shoe-piece. It also includes a pool of water where reeds stand; honey; an ostrich feather; an eland; and the moon. As these characters and elements appear, they strike chords of association in the minds and emotions of all those listening because of the roles they have played from the time of the first story on and through the age-old story-telling process that leads to ultimate communion.

I begin with Mantis as he is the supreme plenipotentiary of creation on Bushman earth; his is the clearest image of the Bushman's acute sense of the infinite in the small, and as such is endowed with powers of creation himself. He is, indeed, so much the child of light that the children of the world appear far wiser in their generation than he. They, like his wife the rock rabbit, his son and grandsons, are constantly reproving him for his apparent foolishness without realizing that it is god-inspired and that that which is still to come always looks impossible in the eyes of what is. He it was, after all, who stole fire to give to the Bushman; he is the Prometheus of that world, and significantly, one of the nicknames conferred on him after my ancestors arrived at the Cape was 'old tinderbox'. With him, the miracle of consciousness – of which fire is our supreme symbol – came into the Bushman's world and set him apart from the animals who, an early story tells us, ran away in great fear from mankind with whom they had been at one, when his first fire was lit. Here already is an example of the great divide, the separation and polarization of life-giving opposites, which consciousness inflicts on man with such a nostalgia for the whole that preceded it. With consciousness, inevitably, came the word, because it was Mantis, it is said, who first gave things their names, declaring, for instance, that 'Your name shall be tortoise and you shall be utterly tortoise to the end of your days'.

All these associations and many more which I have analysed in *The Heart of the Hunter* were alive and active in the imagination of listeners when Mantis walked on to the earthly scene in this story. However strange or absurd his elevation to such a role may appear to men today who have only to see an insect to rush to the nearest chemist for the latest insecticide, it was not strange to the Greeks who recognized his qualifications for such a role and gave him the name 'mantis', seer, which meant he was a prophet of sorts to them as well. Besides, even my ancestors, for all their imperviousness and other inhibitions, were compelled to think of him as an insect at prayer and so not without numinosity. Not surprisingly, he carried for the Bushman a charge of the numinous of the kind Moses experienced, when he saw fire in the burning bush. I do not know what the Bushman name for Mantis meant but I do find it of the highest significance that, among the thousands of Bushman paintings I have examined, I have not found one of Mantis, implying that he, too, did not allow images, painted or graven, to be made of him. Hence it is as a bringer of consciousness and as an instrument of enlarging human awareness that he figures most of all in this story.

Kwammanga, his son-in-law, his future self in the law of creation, is not flesh and blood, not even insect or anything tangible but an element visible at times in the rainbow. Since we know that the rainbow in our Hebraic story was an arc of the covenant set by God in the sky as a sign that he would never flood the world again, never allow unconsciousness on a universal scale to overwhelm consciousness again, it is not surprising that, as son of Mantis, he, too, represents consciousness of a kind. It is consciousness of the beginning in the here and now, and far more circumscribed than the large awareness for whose increase Mantis is uniquely responsible.

He and his sons, all images of Mantis's future selves, are in the business of living out today new stages of consciousness imposed on their reluctant and conservative selves by Mantis; they are the politicians and statesmen, as it were, in the parliament of the totality of Mantis's complex and diversified being; converting Mantis's vision of the impossible into the art of the possible. As more evidence of the Bushman's gift for universality, all this would have been dear to the heart of Goethe, who also thought of the rainbow in a similar way, especially as a natural image of consciousness. As for the two shoe-pieces in the story, they are there as images of man's conscious way through life, his consciously adapted behaviour. Kwammanga's shoe-piece is the image of his role, his influence on the way of man in the restricted here and now; that of Mantis is the image of the greater awareness which compels stone-age man to think beyond the here and now and serve the being to come. As a result, Mantis becomes in most of the stories the great, incorrigible disturber of the peace and social order; the trickster who twists, convulses and confounds fireside complacency and is forever at war with the gravity of human inertia. Although his strange family is forced to obey him, it fears and mistrusts him, complying with his wishes with an air of 'Oh God, what next?' which in many stories was such irresistible comedy for my ancestors. As the fear of the Lord was the wisdom of the Old Testament Lord, so it is with Mantis, and at the end of the long and complex Mantis saga, I have emerged again and again with a searing re-perception of how the love of creator for the created is darkened not only by a separation from the created but also by a lack of reciprocity of love from the created. These stories are full of illustrations of Mantis's love of *all* things but none of an equal reciprocity. It is as if there is, implicit in the way he carries on the task of creation regardless, an assumption that that is precisely what creators are for. Without that thought, I would not have had an inkling of what the story of Job might mean, or that appointment with a cross in Palestine.

219

The pool of water is a symbol of the life-giving and transfigurative energies in the collective unconscious. Just as in the Bible wells, rivers and watering places are the material of miracles and settings for fateful and sacred encounters, so they are in the saga of Mantis in particular, and of stone-age man in general. For instance, it is in such water that Mantis resurrects his son killed in his great war against the baboons, by dipping his dead child's eye – his vision of the future – deep in the pool.

Perhaps most moving of all because it is from a story told with singular delicacy and tenderness, it is in such a pool that a Bushman of the early race, hungry and dispirited, sees the wind that represents the living spirit, spiralling over the stricken wasteland. It lifts an ostrich feather to which one tiny speck of dried blood is clinging and deposits it deep in the pool, where it is transformed into a perfect ostrich chick. The pool in the story to be told is surrounded by reeds, marking it as an area of growth dear not only to the water but to the wind that sings in passing as they sway and swish in the rhythm of its movement, a song of birth, death, resurrection and eternal life-giving change.

The honey, which recurs in many a story, was dearer even to Mantis than to the Bushman for whom it was miraculous and a source of sacramental transubstantiation. The Bushman, the most perceptive and experienced naturalist and botanist Africa ever produced before our coming, had observed the bee faithfully and long, even as Solomon the Great had commanded the men of his day to observe the ant and become wiser in the process. For the Bushman the bee was an image of wisdom and foresight in action; the patience, industry, perseverence, selflessness, attention to minuscule detail, and devotion of all to transcendent value, which was the life of the bee, made a profound impact on the Bushman imagination. Bees and his perma-

220

nent water were, according to my ancestors, almost the only two fixed material elements he was prepared to fight for as for his own life. In going about the business of promoting the welfare of his own highest value, which significantly was feminine, the bee was also an instrument of universal creation, fertilizing the flowers and fruit of his world and transforming their essences into honey. For this pagan African honey, with its wild flavour and texture so translucent with archaic light and made of the essences of the flowers of creation itself, brought sweetness to the stone-age man's palate in a way equivalent to the light of his eye in the night of his spirit. In the logic of an imagination wide open to the wonder of creation, inevitably honey became the ultimate symbol of the wisdom that leads to the sweet-ness of disposition which is a love that transforms and the only source of power that could not corrupt. That this was already so in the beginning is made clear in a story which describes how one of the first deeds of Mantis was to give the animals their different colours and in so doing fixed each colour with honey. He was clearly devoting all the sweetness, the love in his disposition, to the task.

The feather that follows, of course, represents the bird which, in a land so rich in bird life as Africa, is never far from the story-teller's imagination. Plato, who described the mind of man as a cage of birds, would not have marvelled at the fact that for the Bushman, too, the bird represented inspiration, the thoughts that come into the mind of man, winging of their own accord out of the blue of the imagin-ation and demanding to be acknowledged and followed.

One of Klara's first stories to me was of the Bushman hunter who, as a result of just seeing the reflection of a great white bird in the water of a deep blue pool at which he was drinking in the heat of the day, lost all his passion for hunting game. He devoted the rest of a long life to an exhausting and apparently vain quest for the bird which he knew only by its reflection. Close to death, he had travelled far and wide enough to reach the foot of an unscalable mountain, on top of which the bird was reported to roost. Convinced, as he watched the sheer cliff soaring into the blue evening above him, that he would now die without ever seeing the bird itself, he lay down in despair, until suddenly a small voice said: 'Look up!' In the red of the dying day, he saw a lone white feather come floating down to him. He stretched out his hand and grasped it, and in grasping it, I was told, he died content.

When I asked for the name of the bird, Klara told me: 'It has many names but we think of it as the bird of truth'. It has remained a key story of my life and a source of illumination of many obscure things.

The feather in this story may not be a feather of the bird of truth itself but nonetheless the association with it is important because it is also a servant of the living truth that the great white bird symbolizes. It is specifically an ostrich feather, a feather of the bird from which Mantis stole the fire that is consciousness and which he gave to man. As a consequence of the natural precision which characterizes stone-age symbolism, fire, the inspiration which is the image of the source of the greatest transformation of life on earth, could only be represented by the biggest bird of all – a bird, moreover, which was deprived of the gift of flight after the theft of fire as a sign that consciousness had come down from heaven to earth forever.

After the feather, the inspiration: the eland, the greatest of African antelopes, charged with a grandeur of creation in a measure that exceeds all others of its kind no matter how impressive their beauty and grace, is the central element and instrument in the symphonic story. For the Bushman he represented creation in its highest animal form,

222

food for survival in its greatest abundance, and in its most nourishing, reassuring and alchemical measure; so much so that the eland was associated with the miraculous and given a eucharistic role in stone-age culture not accorded to any other animal. He was, I was told, dearest of all to Mantis, and in some stories Mantis is depicted seated between the horns of the eland. In one story told to me in the Kalahari, Mantis is seated between magnetic toes that release sharp electric clicks which echo as the eland walks, magisterial in the silence of the desert, lifting one patent-leather hoof after the other. It is what I have often heard and observed him doing, and in this bleak European scene I ache in my heart for the wonder of it all. It is as if we are being told symbolically by stone-age man that Mantis, positioned between the eland's eyes, directs its seeing so that his vision and the eland's are one; and that, positioned also between the eland's toes, Mantis is showing us that the eland's way is Mantis's way. The symbol could not be more complete and meaningful, and all this is given additional force by the fact that no animal figures more frequently, diversely and beautifully in the rock paintings of Africa than the eland. There is not a phase of his physical existence and his importance to the welfare of stone-age man that is not a subject of rock paintings from the mountains of Natal, the plains and hills of southern Africa through to the Kalahari and on to Namibia. But more significantly still, his numinous character, his eucharistic role, his translation into a bridge between the divine and man is greatest in the Bushman's dances and in the best of his paintings.

I think of one particular painting in this regard, perhaps the most remarkable of all. It is painted on the fragmented and scoured canvas of rock of what was once a great cave in the mountains between Natal and Lesotho. There, in the quiet, a great herd of eland graze at peace, unstalked and unhunted, and move across the rock to the music of a fall of water nearby. But suddenly there rises from among them the awesome shape of two beautifully painted Bushman Titans. Tall as the Bushman always walked in his own imagination, he has never walked as tall as these shapes. The instinctive authority and power of the Titans in the painting left no doubt that they were deliberately raised by the artist out of a passionate longing for a state of being far beyond that on earth below. High above the placid herd a mystical animal is depicted as the goal and food for yet another ascent of the spirit of man. It is in a true sense both a mythological and a mystical painting, and the way the numinous and Pentecostal harmonize with the natural and normal progression of the herd made me tingle all over. Like the story to come which also has an eland at its core, the painting rises fountain-wise in a place of stone-age spirit where man experienced the revelation of the divine.

Finally, there is the moon which he loved as man loves woman. In one of his first stories, I was told, the moon looked down on the people of the early race and saw how afraid they were of dying. Moved in its heart by compassion, the moon summoned the fastest animal nearby, the hare, and commanded: 'Run, tell the people on earth to look at me and know that as I in dying am renewed again, so they in dying will be renewed again.'

The hare in its haste – and in Bushman mythology as in many others, haste was invariably a source of evil – got the message wrong and told the people: 'The moon wants you to look at it and know that unlike it, who in dying is renewed again, you in dying will not be renewed.' The moon was angry and it hit the hare in the lip so hard that it was split, as it remains to this day, as a sign that it bore false witness in a matter of universal truth.

All these instruments combined in the following story of

Mantis and the eland to strike great chords in the memory of stone-age man and swelled as in the climax of a great symphony, soaring to reinforce the urgent music of the spheres beyond the stars.

So this is the story. Once upon a time, Kwammanga took off part of his shoe and threw it away. Mantis picked up the despised piece and took it to the water at a place where the reeds stood. It is as if Mantis is aware already that the spirit renews itself out of what is despised and rejected by our worldly selves. It is an eternal axiom of 'becoming' as expressed in the biblical observation that the stone the builders rejected became the cornerstone of the building. Hence Mantis soaks the piece of worn-out leather (the spent way that needs renewal) in the water (the transfigurative element of the unconscious). He goes back later and finds that the rejected element has already been transformed into a tiny eland and, since it is still small, he leaves it there until it is strong enough to emerge from the water by itself. Then Mantis rejoices, dances and sings to it, and fetches it honey. He summons, in fact, all the love and wisdom at his disposal and rubs the honey into it to make it beautiful, strong, wise and great. Mantis becomes so moved by his creation that he weeps as he fondles it. For the magical number of three nights, he leaves the little eland to grow great within the pool by itself and then returns to call it to come out of the womb of the unconscious onto firm conscious earth. The story says the eland 'rose forth' and came to Mantis in such a manner that the ground resounded with the power and glory of his coming, and Mantis composed and sang for joy a song about it before once more rubbing it down with honey. Only then did he return to rest at his home.

The story proceeds from there to disclose in detail how Mantis's rainbow aspect and grandsons, his future selves, become aware of his creation and in Mantis's absence combine to kill the eland and cut it up for food. Mantis comes upon them in the process and weeps for the eland, but his sorrow, by implication, is not just caused by the killing, as there is no other way in which the eland can be made food not only for the body but for the spirit. He weeps also for his suffering which is being exacted under a clause of the law of creation itself that separates and sets apart the creator and his creation. Mantis is in the role here of a stone-age Moses who can lead others to a promised land of new being which he is not allowed to enter or participate in himself; his bitterness for the moment is extreme and is depicted in a furious argument with the gall of the dead eland.

The gall was one part of an animal that even stone-age man could not swallow. And it seemed for a while as if Mantis would not succeed in swallowing and digesting the gall of the consequences of the separation his creation had forced on him. The gall warns Mantis that if it is pierced and dispersed, it will burst and overwhelm him with the darkness of hate and despair. In the end, however, Mantis pierces the gall which, as threatened, covers him all over so that indeed he can no longer see. The bitterness has become so great that he has no vision left at all and he has to grope along the ground in hate and despair, feeling his way like an eyeless animal. He finds at last an ostrich feather – a flicker of consciousness that was fire in the great bird's keeping. It is enough to brush the last vestige of negation and unconscious resentment out of his eyes and to make conscious the meaning of what Mantis had done intuitively and so make his suffering bearable; since all suffering is bearable once a meaning is discerned within it.

Free in heart and mind again, he throws the feather high up into the sky, committing the flame of light that emancipated him into a permanent light of heaven, calling out to it, as it soars up: 'You must now lie up in the sky. You must henceforth be the moon. You shall shine at night. You shall by your shining light up the darkness for all man. You are the moon, you do fall away, you return to life, when you have fallen away, you give light to all the people.'

In a total recall of the role of this story in my own imagination from childhood over the long random years of a life that is rounding fast, I remembered something I read in my boyhood lying on a dune beside a gleaming Indian Ocean, a mirror of unfathomed sea darkened as by a cat's-paw of wind with reflections of longing to travel then from a halfway to a full house of history and spirit. It was a passage from *Upanishads*, to which Indian friends in Port Natal had directed me. It describes a scene at the court of the great king to which the sage Yajnavalkhya had been summoned.

'By what light,' the king asked him, 'do human beings go out, do they work and return?'

'By the light of the sun,' the sage answers.

'But if the light of the sun is extinguished?'

'By the light of the moon,' the sage replies.

And so question and answer proceed; if the moon is extinguished, then by the starlight; if even the stars are cancelled, by the light of the fire; but if the fire too is quenched, what then, the king finally wants to know.

'By the light of the self,' is the conclusive reply.

I had no doubt that in this story Mantis was teaching the spirit of stone-age man a discovery of the self in which the great sage who never knew them put all his trust as well. For without this moon of renewal to transfigure our partial, bright daytime selves spent under all that is symbolized by the great sun of reason, men shall lose themselves in light as stars are lost in morning even before the nightfall of their

227

time. This moon which lifted Mantis out of hate and black rejection, is an image charged with evocation of the capacities with which life has equipped the human spirit to see through the darkness that falls when his conscious self fails. It is the symbol of all the feminine values, the caring, feeling values, the receptive spirit charged with wonder and hope and the glow, as the shining of the moon, that is intuition and its shy intimations of new being and becoming that make the opaque past, the dark present and obscure future, translucent with inner light, as was the comb of wild African honey that Mantis used to make the eland great and stone-age spirit new.

We live, I wrote at the end of a long desert exploration some thirty years ago, in a sunset hour of time and need the light of this moon of Mantis, this feminine Ariadne soul, which conducts the travel-stained prodigal son of man on a labyrinthine journey to the innermost chamber of his spirit where he meets the 'thou that heals'. Had it not been for the Bushman, I myself would not have the confirmation, the certainty and continuity of hope in the wholeness of an origin and a destination that is one and holy. And I wish I could take each one of these anonymous fragments of those remaining stone-age men and women by the arm and say to them before they vanish: 'Thank you, and please go in the dignity that is your right. You and your fathers were not beasts and cattle but hunters after meaning; painters of animal eucharist and metamorphosis of man on canvasses of rock; tellers of stories that were seeds of new awareness; dancers of dances that restored men to the fellowship of the stars and moon and made them heal one another; and makers of music in which the future sings. They have altogether travelled a way of the truth that would make men free.'

In this, I know, they did not live in vain, however much

the desecrated present denies their children. We need their spirit still. We who loom so large on the scene are not better than they, only more powerful with a power that corrupts us still. It is we who shall have lived in vain unless we follow on from where their footprints are covered over by the wind of the moving spirit that travels the ultimate borders of space and time from which they were redeemed by their story. Woven as it is into a pattern of timeless moments, their story may yet help the redeeming moon in us all on the way to a renewal of life that will make now forever.

Acknowledgement

I owe a very special debt of gratitude to Jane Brewster Bedford for all her imaginative help and editing skills in bringing together this last testament of mine on the role of the story in the mind of man, and its root in the first people of my native country.